DHARMA, ECOLOGY AND WISDOM IN THE THIRD MILLENNIUM

The Author

Henryk Skolimowski is a creator of Eco-philosophy and the author of numerous books on the subject, including *Dancing Shiva in the Ecological Age* and *Ecoyoga*. He published 35 books and over 400 articles. Was educated in Poland, then at Oxford, where he received D. Phil. in philosophy. Taught at various universities, including the University of Michigan (for 21 years.) He has been actively engaged in healing the planet, in spreading the philosophy of sane living and in relating ecology to spirituality, to Dharma, to perennial wisdom.

DHARMA, ECOLOGY AND WISDOM IN THE THIRD MILLENNIUM

Henryk Skolimowski
Professor Emeritus, University of Michigan

CONCEPT PUBLISHING COMPANY, NEW DELHI - 110 059.

ISBN 81-7022-789-5 (HB)

First Published 1999

Published and Printed by
Ashok Kumar Mittal
Concept Publishing Company
A/15-16, Commercial Block, Mohan Garden,
New Delhi -110 059 (India)

PREFACE

In many spiritual traditions - Hinduism, Buddhism, and Jainism, but also in Christianity and Islam - beautiful words were spoken in praising the glory of nature. Yet the deep meaning of these words have been forgotten and our consciousness is no longer shaped by the high precepts of the Vedas and other scriptures. Instead, our consciousness and action have been shaped by the commands and imperatives of how to manipulate nature to our advantage, often with disastrous consequences. Therefore, a radical dusting off is required, really a quiet spiritual revolution, to bring out the seeds of ecological consciousness and ecological Dharma to full fruition.

Dharma has many aspects, many layers, many depths. In our times Dharma must be extended to include our care for Mother Earth. As we enter the New Millennium, we have to wake up: so much is required of us to make this millennium one of sanity, harmony and peace. One of the changes we need to make is within ourselves, namely, to realize that many of the old venerable precepts will have to be given a new lease of life. Thus Dharma has recently been given a new dimension as Eco-Dharma

Eco-Dharma is a *new awareness* of what our present world and future generations require for a meaningful existence.

Eco-Dharma is a call to *action* to protect the beauty of the physical world which is our cradle, our vessel, our nurturer, the source of our spiritual sustenance.

Eco-Dharma suggests and proposes a profoundly new interpretation of old scriptures which must be seen as the hymns to the glory of all creation but also invitations to the participatory dance, in which the Atman enshrines Brahman by truly taking care of its well-being — including this world. Yes, we are contributing to the well-being of God. The main aim of Eco-Dharma is to make ourselves sacred while taking all creation with us.

The ecological and the spiritual are one. Eco-Dharma unites the world of ancient rishis with the world of future generations which will live in a world healed and recovered from its present wounds. Eco-Dharma is a new hope for the new millennium.

We have learnt from earlier philosophers that action without reflection is blind, while reflection without action is impotent. We need to derive an appropriate lesson from this teaching. We should thus be perfectly aware that so much action, in our present world, is unguided and un-illumined, and frequently leads to destruction. We should also be perfectly aware that so much abstract thought consists of merely scholastic exercises, which help nobody and only exhaust the mind.

However, there are some forms of reflections, which are illuminating forms of Logos, which combine deep understanding with the imperative of action. Eco-Dharma is such a form of reflection. It is so charged with the energy of right understanding, so deeply illumined with the awareness of what is right and what is wrong and what needs to be done that its true understanding is the beginning of action and its complete understanding is the completion of action.

Eco-Dharma as such does nothing, but it enables everything. For it is this special energy, this special light of understanding, this penetrating vision which, through the power of Logos combined with the divine light which gives us direction, as well as support and sustenance in whatever we do.

Eco-Dharma inspires, guides and enables, is this form of charged and luminous energy of understanding which, in virtue of being what it is, creates right action, furthermore, creates harmony in the world and bliss in the human heart.

Eco-Dharma informs us that to understand what it means is to immediately act on its behalf — in restoring the earth to its balance and radiance, and in restoring ourselves to our true harmony and glory. The inner temple and the outer temples are aspects of each other, are simply one. We, the keepers of Eco-Dharma, understand this truth very well and act accordingly.

Once we understand that traditional Dharma needs to be re-examined, deepened and given a new dimension, this immediately leads to the awareness that traditional Karma is in need of re-examination; and so it is with traditional yoga. They all need a new lease of life, a new dimension. Equally our notion of politics and of ethics need to be re-examined through the prism of the imperative of the survival of the earth. This whole process finally leads us to new thinking and new perception, without which we can hardly survive. Our Dharma for the Third Millennium is to understand that it is our duty to change the multitude. Unless everything is changed, nothing will be changed.

This little treatise is a guide how we can renew ourselves - not in a superficial way, but by going to the foundations. This book is especially addressed to ecology minded people to make them aware that there is more to ecology than fighting for the preservation of the physical environment. Ecology is a spiritual quest.

This book is equally addressed to spiritually minded people and spiritual communities to make them aware that there is much more to Dharma and to religious duty than can be found is traditional scriptures. Our new religious responsibility is to save the world and all creation. And, of course, this book is addressed to all thinking people to make them aware that there is an exquisite connection between the ancient idea of Dharma (religion) and the new idea of ecology.

CONTENTS

Chapter 1

Philosophy, Dharma, Ecology

Philosophy

Philosophy has travelled through many roads. At times it attempted to scale the most demanding high altitude paths leading to heaven. It then became theology - the search for God. At other times it explored the chambers and galleries of the palace of human wisdom. This is the most classic road of philosophy, epitomized by its very name 'philo-sophia', a love of wisdom. Sometimes it was satisfied with being the synthesis of knowledge. Unmindful of wisdom, it then wanted to be the queen of the sciences - distilling what it thought was most essential in human knowledge. Sometimes, particularly in the 20th century, it had the ambition of being a science, as precise as physics and mathematics; hence it couched itself in the language of mathematical logic.

Philosophy, particularly as envisaged by Socrates and Plato, was also the quest for a meaningful life, for a worth while life. This quest has been gradually eliminated from the course of Western philosophy. But this quest has never been abandoned within the Indian tradition, within which philosophy has often been pursued as a path of 'Moksha' (liberation), as a guide to human destiny. This has been the strength of the Indian tradition and its philosophy. This ideal of philosophy - as Moksha - is quite close to the meaning of the term Dharma.

Although Dharma has many shades of meaning its conception as a guide on the path of right duty is quite essential. Equally essential is the meaning of Dharma as spelling out our obligation to become liberated. These forms of Dharma which illumine for us the path of our destiny and make us aware that it is our duty to pursue them, are essentially forms of philosophy.

Thus Dharma is a form of philosophy. For what else can it be? It is usually regarded as something apart from philosophy, as something deeper, as a voice of heaven. But how can you understand this voice, how can you understand its depth, if not through your philosophical faculties? Philosophy does not need to be shallow. And Dharma is not necessarily always deep. Some forms of Dharma are shallow. The understanding of the shallowness or the depth of philosophy or of Dharma, for that manner is essentially philosophical understanding. Thus there is a philosophical imprint on all forms of Dharma.

Yet this is not how Dharma is usually conceived. It is often received as something immediate, as commands from Heaven, as a voice of our destiny or an inner declaration of who we are and what is our mission. Even if it were so, we need to notice that : if Dharma is a voice of Heaven, then the heavens are very philosophical; if Dharma is a voice of deities, these deities are very philosophical; if Dharma is a voice of our inner conscience, this conscience is very philosophical. Understanding Dharma is not a mindless process. It requires a deep philosophical sensitivity, but not necessarily a wealth of philosophical knowledge. It requires an awareness of the wonderful intricacies of human destiny and of the sense of belonging to the larger cosmos - even if this awareness is not explicitly articulated in the individual's mind.

Why would you follow any path of Dharma if deep down you did not understand that - in spite of its thorns - it is a beautiful path. A path of duty is a path of beauty. It is a philosophical path, a path of wisdom - whether one is clearly aware of this or not. Dharma is this wonderful invention of the human mind which can inspire simple people to a philosophical life. A system of thought which can make simple people to embrace a philosophy is certainly a wonderful achievement of human creativity. The Indian tradition is to be congratulated on this score.

Dharma

As you understand so you act. The higher your understanding the higher your Dharma. The lower your understanding the lower your Dharma. Creatures with no understanding have no Dharma. They follow their instincts and their animal urges. It clearly follows that Dharma is a result of and a companion of understanding. But not any kind of understanding. When you explain the relationship of physical facts to each other, this understanding does not lead to any

Dharma.

Dharma is a daughter of understanding in the world which has purpose and meaning. Dharma is a meaning. Dharma is purpose. Without meaning and purpose, without understanding and wisdom, Dharma would be some kind of blind groping, meaningless gestures of an actor who frantically frets his hour upon the stage and then is seen no more. The higher a being you are, the more luminous is your understanding of the subtle intricacies of Dharma - even if it is not a verbal understanding.

Lord Shiva was continuously vigilant, constantly ready to be of help in maintaining the order of things which might have crumbled without him. Also, Lord Krishna, as is explained in the Gita, must be constantly vigilant, cannot rest even for one minute; for if he does, the whole world might turn to chaos.

We are the messengers of Shiva and Krishna. Nay, we are their embodiments and their energy. The more clearly we grasp it the more we become like them - in magnanimity, power, insight, love and understanding. But we need to have courage - to grasp it and to live it. This courage is a form of understanding. Thus the circle closes : we need courage to increase understanding. As our understanding increases, so our courage does. Then we are capable of performing our higher Dharmas. There is a direct correlation between deeper understanding and being called to perform higher dharmas.

And yet, in our times, we do not expect learned scholars to understand the realms of higher Dharma. Although their knowledge is so vast, their understanding is so small. The forms of bookish understanding are not the ones that lead to understanding the purpose and meaning of the universe and of our own life. The roads of bookish understanding are not the roads to the energy of Krishna and Shiva.

The light of understanding is such a peculiar thing. It does not come with the cramming of more and more bookish knowledge into your head. Yes, the light is there to be seen. But it is now more obscured than in previous times. We therefore require a special insight and special energy to penetrate the clouds of this obscurity - in order to see our purpose and our destiny. We also need new insights to see our new responsibilities, new realms of our Dharma. Those who are most sensitive and seeing, now perceive that the most important aspects of our present Dharma is saving the Earth.

Ecology

The idea of Ecology has been around us for a quarter of a century. We have become used to it. We consider its ramifications good, namely, to have clean air, clean water, clean soil. But ecology is much deeper and much more far reaching than cleaning the polluted physical environment. Yes, cleaning the polluted physical environment is very important. But it is only a small part of the task; yes, a *small* part. For what is ultimately responsible for the polluted planet is not dirty technologies but polluted minds - careless, unseeing, alienated. Contaminated minds produce, almost of necessity, contaminated environments.

The present condition of humanity is forlorn as we dwell in polluted physical environment, in polluted mental environments, in polluted spiritual environments. We need to purify ourselves in so many ways. Traditional poojas are insufficient. Our minds so often resemble a garbage container rather than a beautiful shining shrine of God. The ecology of mind is still in its infancy. Let us be aware that we need to purify our mind not through some old fashion rituals, but through something much more drastic but also more lasting. We need to change the whole structure of our consciousness which is programmed to manipulation, to mechanistic thinking, to an instrumental treatment of people and nature. In effect, we need to create the reverential mind (which I have discussed at length in *Living Philosophy*, Penguin, 1992).

The contaminated mechanistic mind has weakened (and sometimes contaminated) the sources of our spiritual life. This mind has separated us from the sacred. Hence, our spiritual life has been weakened - both on the individual level and on the level of whole cultures. By allowing to contaminate and garbagize your mind, you dim your intelligence and blunt your sensitivities, and thus make your life less radiant and more obtuse; ultimately, you diminish yourself as a person. This point is of great importance but usually unappreciated.

We rarely realize that the contaminated physical environment leaves behind its shadow which is contaminated mental and spiritual environments. A true work of ecology is healing all the three environments simultaneously : physical, mental and spiritual. Thus, our Dharma must be extended and deepened to include new realms.

In our times the most important task is to clean the earth, to cleanse ourselves from mental pollution. Our minds are as polluted as our bodies, as is our air, our rivers, our soil. Preserving the continuity of the earth and the integrity of our souls are very important aspects of our present Dharma.

Thus Dharma acquires a distinctly green or ecological dimension. Whatever divides us (our cultures, our tongues, our religions, our economic systems) one thing that unites us is ecology - the care for the earth, the care for future generations, the care for the well being of all sentient beings.

It is not sufficient nowadays to care for yourself, for your spiritual well being, for your religious community. You must extend this care to the entire earth - for this is your dwelling, your temple, your sangha, your vessel in which spiritual attainments can be perfected on your way to Bodhisattva and then to the Buddha.

It we lose the environment, if we destroy the earth, we lose God, we then destroy the grounds for all other possibilities, for becoming spiritual beings and ultimately enlightened beings. Previous Buddhas, including Gautama, were not so aware of the frailty of the planet earth as the ground for cultivating our humanity and our spirituality. For to say it once more, if this ground is denied, our spiritual journey comes to an end.

Hence the importance of Ecological Dharma - not only for the preservation of the earth as such, but for the preservation of the *conditions* which enable us to become human, thus enable us to follow the path of the Buddha or the path of Shiva or the path of Krishna; or whatever spiritual path we have chosen to follow. Seen in this light, ecological Dharma is of importance second to none! If you are a spiritual person, you must care about ecology for its is your spiritual cradle. In our times the ecological and the spiritual become one. To revere the Buddha or Krishna is to work for the salvation and healing of the planet.

True prayer and true meditation in our time becomes ecological prayer - such a form of meditation and action which helps to heal the planet, which helps to heal other human beings, which helps to heal all other beings - including the forests, soil and polluted rivers. This new form of redemption - ecological redemption is truly universal in nature. It is based on universal compassion towards all beings - threatened by man's excessive technological activities. To see what is most important for the well being of all sentient beings (and semi-sentient beings such as the soil and forests), to see what is most important for our inner peace and our ascent towards the Buddha, we need a new perspective

- the Ecological Perspective, and a new form of Dharma
- Ecological Dharma.

The Dharma of Ecological Philosophy

Much of the present teaching of both Hinduism and Buddhism is steeped in the past. And much of it is a repetition of old dogmas. Non-attachment is (by and large) a noble and liberating principle. But we need to re-examine its meaning in view of the importance of Ecological Dharma. We cannot be too detached from the earth. We need to *cling to the earth* - though the phrase may alarm some orthodox Hindus or Buddhists. To care for the earth, to work for its healing and salvation means to be attached to the earth, though we may say that it is not a selfish attachment. The meaning of ecological Dharma calls for a new reflection on, and indeed a significant revision of some ancient spiritual traditions, including Buddhism, Hinduism and Christianity.

Ecological Dharma informs us that the ecological reconstruction, working close to nature, bringing back labour intensive occupations, in general, working for the ecological catharsis, is the road which leads us to the fold of right livelihood. Thus, Ecological Dharma appears to be an essential vehicle to bring us back to right livelihood which is so essential to our spiritual wellbeing. Unless we find the road reconnecting us with right livelihood - not only for a select few but for countless millions - we cannot claim that our spiritual message is relevant to our times. Wrong livelihood is destroying people's souls and is undermining the sustainability of the planet.

What is the specific Dharma of Ecological Philosophy? It is to reassure us that philosophy is not dead; that in fact, it has a most important role to play, at this particular time, when wisdom has been replaced by information. Another aspect of the Dharma of Eco-Philosophy is moral guidance. Modernism and Post-modernism have disintegrated in the quick sand of nihilism and moral confusion. Traditional philosophy has not been able to help us in combating this moral decay. Ecological philosophy proposes new imperatives for moral actions and for the moral regeneration of the individual. The moral regeneration is a most important part of our spiritual regeneration.

Yet another and perhaps the most important aspect of the Dharma of Eco-Philosophy, is to make us understand that the ecology of mind, the ecology of the spirit, and the ecology of physical environment are aspects of each other; and that the pollution of physical environment inevitably leads to the pollution of the mind and the spirit. This understanding also informs us that the degradation of physical environment is a consequence of the polluted minds and sullied souls.

Ecological Philosophy is itself a form of Dharma. Once you understand things in their true connections, once you see them in their true light, you must act accordingly - in order to bring them back to a right alignment. To understand aright is to act aright. The Dharma of Ecological Philosophy tells you that you must put your own house in order. The Dharma of Ecological Philosophy also instructs us that we must be teachers - all of us. We must spread the necessary light, in spite of all the obstacles and the crippling influence of the structures of darkness. Right education is the foundation of right awareness, which in turn is the foundation of all our thinking and of our action. Right education is the right implementation of the right values. An ancient Chinese expression says : if you are preparing for one year, plant rice; if you are preparing for 25 years, plant the trees; if you are preparing for 100 years, plant right education.

Summary

The Dharma of ecological philosophy, in a nutshell, is singing the right song with the unfolding universe which is so beautiful but also fraught with so many dangers and pitfalls. May *we have enough courage to bear the light which is required of us to make the universe luminous and kind.*

Our times call for new resources of imagination, for new resources of inner power to meet the unprecedented peril to the life of the planet and to our own spiritual lives. The two are aspects of each other. A new ecological Dharma is called for. This Dharma required of us to be passionately attached to the earth, which of course does not mean the childish clinging to material possessions and to consumption.

The practice of universal compassion in our times requires the work of the ecological reconstruction and ecological healing unprecedented in history. As the ecological crisis has brought about an enormous sea of new suffering, the ecological cleansing is the vehicle of the cessation of suffering. *Ecology is the noble truth of our times. Eco-philosophy is the Dharma of our times.*

Literature

Henryk Skolimowski, *Dancing Shiva in the Ecological Age*, Clarion Press, New Delhi, 1991; Indian Institute of Ecology and Environment, New Delhi, 1995.

- Living Philosophy, Eco-philosophy as a Tree of Life, Penguin, London, 1992.
- A Sacred Place to Dwell, Element Books, U.K. 1993.
- The Participatory Mind, A New Theory of Knowledge and of the Universe, Penguin, London, 1994.
- Eco-Yoga, Practice and Meditations for Walking in Beauty on The Earth, Gaia Books, London, 1994.

Chapter 2

The Meaning of Karma From the Ecological Perspective

T.S. Eliot - An Unheralded Prophet of the Ecological Epoch.

T.S. Eliot is known as a poet. And mainly as a poet of the sardonic gloom and of existential malaise. On a deeper level, however, Eliot reveals himself as a precursor of the ecological epoch. His prophetic visions heralding the age of ecology are not explicit. However, when we read him aright, not by concentrating on what he denounces, but by revealing what he dearly cherishes, the message is clear.

I have often quoted these three lines :

Where is the Life we have lost in living ?
Where is the wisdom we have lost in knowledge ?
Where is the knowledge we have lost in information ?

These lines reveal powerfully the tragic predicament of Western knowledge which is so potent and so powerful but ultimately so empty and so futile, for it has traded wisdom for information and the meaning of life for consumption. Any philosophy worthy of the 21st century must be guided by wisdom and not by merely logic or by a compendium of scientific facts and theories.

Here is another revealing vista of Eliot :

Of all you have done in the past,
You eat the fruit
Either rotten or ripe

Eliot's poetic incantations conceal deep moral insights. Yet we prefer to be enchanted by the power of poetry as we glide over its moral substratum. The 20th century has not been a moral age. It has been a nihilistic age. For this reason the proponents of the high moral road had to maintain a low profile. The prophets of high greed however have been very vocal and highly visible. Many centuries ago, Eurepides had said :

He who rightly with necessity
Complies with things divine
We count him skilled and wise.

The message is simpler than that of Eliot. Moreover, it is expressed in a positive vein : We salute those who have the courage to follow the divine road. In Eliot, the message is expressed cryptically, emphasizing the negative consequences of bad deeds.

The 20th century has not had the courage of positive visions. The best thinkers have been dancing a tortuous dance of self effacement, not daring to be positive. Instead, they tried to show how 'sophisticated' they were by deriding everything beautiful and noble and by despising higher moral values.

The ecological paradigm is changing it all. It has maintained that it is right and proper to believe in things noble. It is right to comply with things divine, as Eurepides proposed. The positive vision is not a weakness of smaller minds or a prerogative of naive minds, but an expression of courage and vibrancy of one's being. The ecological paradigm challenges the pitifully barren vision of those shallow proponents of material progress who believed in knowledge without wisdom.

I will now show how relevant T.S. Eliot is for our understanding of new extensions of Karma, which I call Ecological Karma. He writes :

A wrong attitude to nature
Implies somewhere a wrong attitude to God
And the consequence is an inevitable doom.

This precept should have been studied by ecologists and religious people alike. But it hasn't been. Eliot is not considered to be a poet relevant to ecology. On the other hand, religious people find him an awkward companion. Let us examine more closely Eliot's precept. For the principle of Eco-karma is hiding there.

How can it be that a wrong attitude to nature can bring about an inevitable doom? Eliot does not explain. Rather he feels it in his bones. For this reason he says rather tentatively :

> A wrong attitude to nature
> *Implies somewhere* a wrong attitude to God.

For the religious peoples of the traditional variety, such a statement does not make sense. The ecologists missed it altogether.

However, within the ecological perspective Eliot's contention makes perfect sense. All things are connected, are parts of the same web of life. A wrong attitude to nature is a desecration of the web itself. Only when we have created a new coherent picture of the earth as a seamless web, in which all parts are interconnected, and indeed aspects of the sacred tapestry; only when we have evolved the image of Gaia as living Earth, extremely resilient but very fragile, only then can we make a full and vibrant sense of Eliot's contention.

Thus, the principle of Eco-karma, a new moral principle which we have felt in our bones, is articulated. When spelled out this principle asserts that it is our duty and responsibility to safeguard Mother Earth and all the ecological habitats as it is our duty to respect and cherish the lives of our brothers and sisters of the human family. Violation of the Earth and of any part of its web is no less a crime than doing violence to individual human beings.

Eco-karma reminds us : be aware of your interconnections with all the visible and breathing cosmos. Nature supports you in countless ways. You have the responsibility and duty to revere her - out of your respect for all creation, out of your respect for the divine, out of your respect for yourself. You have the responsibility to maintain the integrity of the divine. For all is divine.

Another message of Eco-karma is as follows. To be fully aware of yourself is to take the responsibility for all the links which connect you with this amazingly rich and mysterious world. At one point your awareness of the glory of it all becomes a moral responsibility for it all. This is a new layer added to the meaning of traditional karma.

Eco-karma is enlarging the traditional meaning of karma in yet another way. We need to be aware not only of our *individual* karma but of our collective karma - as a society and the human race. Eco-karma insists that we have a responsibility as a *whole species* to take care of the Earth and of other beings. Otherwise the consequences may be inevitable doom.

We can now see that Eco-karma represents also an enlarged principle of Christianity and of Judaism and of Islam : "As you sow, so you reap." The proper formulation of this karmic principle should include the consequences of our action toward nature and toward other beings. Bad karma are those harmful deeds, done to others, which ultimately effect us adversely. A deeper reflection immediately informs us that a wretched treatment of nature, or the elimination of other species by thousands, is bound to bring a bitter harvest to ourselves, and the consequence may be inevitable doom. The principle of Eco-karma is thus sharpening the awareness of our moral responsibility in the universe not limited to humans only.

We have enlarged the meaning of Karma in two ways. The first of these ways is by seeing that between the human individual and God there are many stages which have karmic consequence. We have responsibilities for all these stages-in-between, including taking care of the earth, of other beings, of future generations. While taking care of these stages and attempting to accumulate positive karma, we are not forgetting about God, about our responsibility to the divine, about our inner God. But we now see this ultimate responsibility in a much boarder context.

The second way of enlarging traditional meaning of karma is by seeing that we do not only have individual responsibilities but also collective responsibilities. We are thus co-responsible for collective karma of our society and of the human race. We carry on our shoulders and in our society and of the human race. We carry on our shoulders and in our hearts collective karma for the devastation of nature, of other beings, of aboriginal people. We are not personally responsible for maltreatment of these beings. Yet we carry collective karma on our shoulders and in our consciousness. We may present the two models of karma by means of two diagrams.

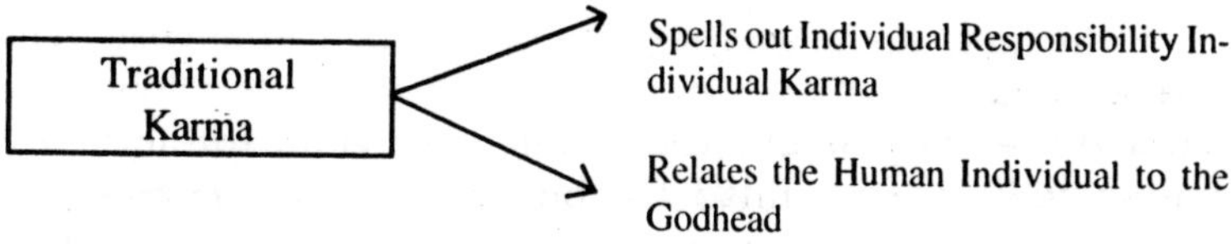

Diagram 1

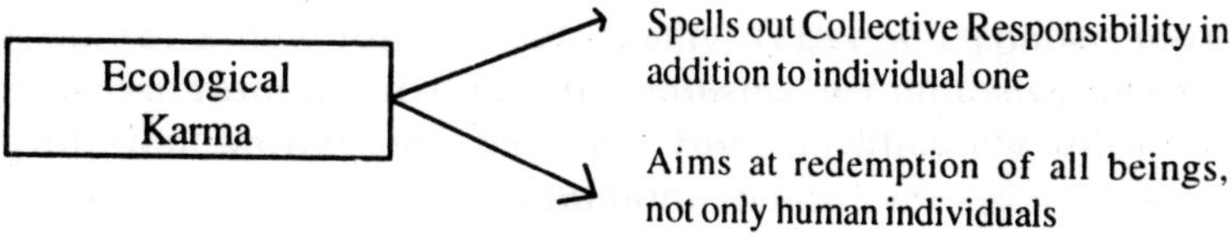

Diagram 2

Why Have We Overlooked the Significance of Eco-Karma?

We have neglected to articulate Eco-karma for at least two important reasons. One is that in pre-historic cultures there was no need for this articulation. People were so woven into the web of nature that they quite naturally protected it as a part of their outer skin. The second reason is more recent. When organized religions emerged, particularly monotheistic ones, people focused their entire attention on the relationship of the human to Deity. Moral laws were then articulated along the religious lines. Eco-karma was missed as a moral principle by divine default. The deities, as it were, did not want to consider nature on the level of importance equal to them. Let us discuss these two reasons in some details.

Early man lived in the state of trance. He was so wrapped in the texture of nature, of the cosmos, of the divine forces that he was hardly conscious of where the human ends and nature begins; also hardly aware at what point natural forces assumed the divine and cosmic dimensions. What was natural, what was cosmic, what was divine was not so clearly distinguishable. For so often natural forces were endowed with divine attributes. In this primordial unity, it was quite natural and indeed inevitable, not to separate the overwhelming flow surrounding the human into people, nature and divinity but to live it all as an unbroken stream of one seamless experience.

In fact, there was no choice to do it otherwise. The consciousness had not yet emerged which would allow us to separate, to chop, to atomize. In this sense early man lived in a trance. All was one. The communication with other beings of the cosmos was perfect, natural, an inherent aspects of how things were. Human consciousness did not need to sacralize nature; specifically it did not need to establish a moral law enunciating the sanctity of nature. Nature was enshrined by virtue of the prevailing cosmology. It was truly a state of naive innocence - until cultures emerged and started reflecting, articulating, establishing moral laws.

We have said earlier that the first moral laws were couched in the religious language. The conception of the moral law, as the edicts from God and heaven, has dominated our moral horizons for millennia, in fact until modern times. Only with Immannual Kant we witness the radical shift : "The starry heaven above you and the moral law within you."

Between the time of the primordial enchantment with the natural world and the philosophy of Immannual Kant a lot has happened. Human consciousness has been articulating itself. Cultures have become more and more refined. The process of self reflection has gradually lead to self doubt; until finally it has arrived at nihilistic skepticism doubting everything : "I doubt therefore I am." The original innocence has been lost. Humans have acquired a distinctive sense of self-consciousness and a distinctive sense of separation from nature.

The acquisition of the distinctive sense of self-consciousness and of one's uniqueness (already in Greek times; let us remember Protagoras: "Man is the measure of all things") is a triumph of human consciousness arising. But it also signifies the fall from grace, the grace of original innocence, the grace of the primordial unity of the human with the surrounding universe.

The process of articulation of self-consciousness and of the sense of human autonomy grows even further in the post-Renaissance time under the aegis of the mechanistic world view. In this period man seeks further liberation. This time from the impositions and dogmas of religious orthodoxies. We wished to abolish the tyranny of God in order to increase further our autonomy. But this also signifies a further fall from grace. Enmeshed by our scientific inventions we have lost our way in the technological jungle. In the process we have lost the sacred and alienated ourselves from nature and from ourselves.

With hindsight we can now see the immaturity of the so-called civilized man. While he was rushing from one action to another, exploring and conquering, he was not quite clearly seeing what he was doing. We can also see the immaturity of organized religions, as they pitted people against people, and as they allowed humans to savage nature and other beings. Religions have too often been exclusive, jealous, overpossessive. They established a special pact with the humans at the expense of other beings of the cosmos. The humans were kidnapped from the family of living beings and made to serve demanding and exclusive gods. This has produced bad karma - for the whole living family. We are now trying to rectify the situation. We realize that healing the Earth is part of our new Dharma, part of our new responsibility to overcome the past bad karma.

The ecological age represents a deliberate effort to establish a new unity with nature and with other beings. It is not a return to the original unity. Such returns are not possible. It is a new unity which transcends the present atomizing and manipulative consciousness in favour of ecological consciousness. It is a new way of resacralizing the world while living in a state of continuous reverence.

Eco-karma informs us that after the fall from original naive grace, we can consciously and deliberately build a new form of grace - the harmony with nature and with all creation built on the foundation of a new moral imperative. We have to establish this harmony because it is in accordance with the cosmic law, namely that all things must be in balance and harmoniously support each other. While this cosmic law was subconsciously upheld in ancient times, we can now consciously and deliberately articulate it as the prerogative of our maturity. Eco-karma celebrates the newly gained consciousness of oneness of all things in the new historic context. Eco-karma is a consequence of the ecological world view. indeed a mature daughter of it.

We have a choice of either continuing with a wrong attitude to nature which leads to inevitable doom, or of embarking on the path of Eco-karma which leads to healing and salvation. In opting out for the ecological world view we have chosen the latter. This is not only a choice of some individuals. This is a choice expressing evolutionary wisdom.

The Indian Tradition

A few words need to be said about karma within the Indian tradition. After all, karma is an Indian term and the Indian tradition has been most articulate about it. Yet the Indian tradition does not have a monopoly on the term. Nor should it be assumed that because the Indian culture (including Hinduism, Buddhism, and Jainism) used the term for millennia we know all that is to be known about karma and no fresh insights are warranted.

Within the Indian tradition, karma has been guided by Divine Providence. This Divine Providence is exemplified, for instance by the *Bhagavad Gita*, or by the sublime discourses of the *Upanishads*, concerning the relationships between the Brahman and the Atman. Yet one wonders after a while whether this guidance has not per chance been too divine; just like in Christianity whereby the moral sin, the closest approximation to karma, is determined solely by the religious context - of man's relationship to God - while man's other responsibilities have been obscured.

The conception of sin and, by implication, of the meaning of karma in the Christian tradition is overwhelmingly determined by old commandments and too little by the new awareness of man's responsibility to nature and other beings; including other human beings outside our own religious traditions. It is frightening to think how many religious wars were fought for the sake of maintaining *our* image of god; how many millions of people were killed in a brutal way in these wars; and what devastation of the land occurred in the process. It is painful to think what kind of karma was the residue of this whole process.

The Hindu tradition so often articulates the relationship between the Atman and the Brahman. The true wisdom is meant to be this kind of vision which enables the individual (Atman) to unite with the absolute (Brahman). We shall agree that this is a

High Road, highly commendable and lauded in all periods of history. Yet we should also remember that our world is so versatile and that between the Atman and Brahman there are many lands to travel through. That is what universal karma signifies. We must make peace in each of these lands we travel through before we reach the ultimate land of light - Brahman.

Moreover, if it is true that all the universe is sacred, then every land we travel through is sacred. We need to pass through each accumulating good karma; and harm none. For harming any land in between, whether these be the people who are of lower status than we are, or ecological habitats, or animals, we harm ourselves, we harm Atman within; in a subtle way we also harm Brahman because we arrive at Brahman not fully clean.

To have a clear awareness of one's relationship to Brahman (or to God) is a mark of high consciousness. Not to be fully aware that passing through the various lands on the way to Brahman involves acts and actions which have karmic consequence is a form of arrogance and hubris. "Of all you have done in the past, you eat the fruit...." At times the Indian tradition is too high minded in forgetting about everything else, save the link between the Atman and Brahman.

We shall emphasize that we are not abandoning or diminishing the past understanding of karma. On the contrary, we are broadening and deepening it so that we can be rightly informed and guided in this difficult age fraught with torturous and unprecedented complexity.

It is a joy to follow the right karma, even if it outlines a path paved with difficulties. We want to know what is right and proper for ourselves and for future generations. Sustainable life should be guided by sustainable karma. We don't want to stumble in confusion and uncertainties. For this produces bad karma. The residue of the mind's confusion is a life lived in fog.

It is a joy to heal others, to heal Mother Earth - to clean, to mend, to purify. We must not be too centered on ourselves. A virtuous path of life is not a narrow lane which joins us directly with deity. It is a broad road which includes so many other beings.

Medicine men and women are highly respected in all traditional societies. They are a living symbol of healing, cleansing, repairing; bringing things to a right orbit again. We are - all of us - now called to join the ranks of the ancient 'shamans' who tirelessly worked for the benefit of all. We are called to join the ranks of Bodhisattvas. We possess the necessary powers within ourselves. We need to bring out these powers from their hiding places and make them blossom. Whether we call this new path Eco-Karma, or a labour of love, or a cosmic necessity, or a Divine Dharma, let us follow it with joy and pride, remembering with Euripides:

Who rightly with necessity
Complies in things divine
We count him skilled and wise.

Chapter 3

From Yoga to Eco-Yoga to Mahayoga

Why Yoga?

We don't know exactly what our ancestors were like 10,000 years ago. We may be certain however that they were far more meditative than we are at present. There was nowhere to rush to. And those great forests they lived in, were like enormous temples, nursing them in the sanctuaries of their silence. The endless hours they spent in nature, in primordial forests, were beautiful forms of meditations.

As civilizations develop, people find the need for special exercises. In ancient Greece the ideal was : a healthy spirit in a healthy body. The ideal of harmony was all pervading in all walks of life and every form of human endeavour. Hence the invention of the institution of *Gymnasion,* a special place where young men met to perform bodily exercises. After these exercise were done, it was quite common to recite poetry and discuss philosophy - as we learn from the dialogues of Plato.

The idea of purposeful physical exercises found its apogee in the Olympic Games, established already in 776 B.C.E. The Olympics combined in an ingenious way two important quests : the need to express one's competitive nature in such a way that competition does not result in aggression and violence. The Olympics presented a very civilized way to channel the restless energy of young men and at the same time allowed their competitive/combative spirit to find an outlet in a harmless and 'democratic' way.

Now, as time went on, and particularly when the Olympics were reintroduced in 1896 in Athens, the Games became increasingly specialized. The physical training of the body, gradually turned the competing humans into extremely specialized physical machines. The ideal of using the Olympics to bring harmony and balance to the human being became lost. This is then the Western story. The search for balance and harmony led the Greeks to invent the *Gymnasion* and to introduce the Olympic Games. In pursuing the Olympics, we began to overspecialize. In chasing for the records, we have pushed the human body to its limits and beyond. In the process, we have lost the ideal of balance and harmony.

The story is altogether different in India. The ancient Hindus also found the need for special bodily exercise. These exercises are called yoga. Yet the pursuit of yoga did not lead to the over-obsession with the physical capacities of the body. The pursuit of yoga led to the path of inner perfection. There are no limits to inner peace. There are no spiritual limits. For this reason, the quest of yoga turned out to be far more significant than the array of bodily exercise of Western culture. Yoga has proven to be a wonderful instrument for achieving and maintaining inner balance and harmony. We turn to yoga and find it so helpful not because it is now fashionable to do so but because yoga (and other spiritual exercises that go with it) have shown themselves far more enduring and of greater significance than the available exercises of the West.

Why is yoga important in our times? Because we are bundles of nerves, a very stressed and unhealthy people. Mental illness abounds; suicide, aggression, murder, rape, paranoia are reaching record heights. All these are the abnormal manifestation of our human nature, a clear indication that we are mentally out of balance. But life loves life. Health is a natural condition of humans. Thus, we intuitively gravitate to the sources of balance and health.

As we are beginning to listen to the voice of our spirit more and more attentively, we find the spiritual wisdom of Indian yoga (and of their meditations) very appealing and helpful. I do not wish to eulogize the Indian tradition at the expense of other spiritual traditions. There is a wealth of spiritual wisdom of Christianity and in Judaism. There are special spiritual exercises leading to inner peace in each. However, these exercises are not as well articulated and not clearly relevant to our present life as are the exercises of the Indian tradition, which is enomorously rich and very sophisticated.

Why Eco-Yoga ?

Is there such a thing as Eco-Yoga ? Yes, there is. I will relate to you how it came about. In 1981 I published a book entitled *Eco-Philosophy, Designing New Tactics for Living*, which was the first systematic tract outlining the field of Eco-Philosophy. A few months after the book was published, I had a conversation on the subject of Eco-Philosophy with a good friend of mine, Leonidas Ossetynski, in Hollywood, California. He was at that time an active actor and a Director of a school for actors. I explained to him the major ideas of my book while he was listening attentively. He really could listen well. I knew he was absorbing my ideas completely. Then he took a deep breath and asked me an unexpected question: "What kind of exercise are you going to give them?" "What exercises ?" I responded, "I am not training actors. I am a philosopher, building a new system".

He smiled gently and said pensively : "You don't understand. If you give people only ideas, they will stay in the abstract part of their coconut. These ideas will not be integrated with people's lives. You need to devise exercises which will translate ideas into living experiences, into the layers of their being so that they can live these ideas and not only think about them. Thinking about ideas is one thing. Living them - quite another."

Somehow I thought his challenge impertinent. Yet deep down I felt it to be very pertinent. Indian systems of thought have historically combined reflection with yoga beautifully. But in Western philosophy there has been no such thing.

During the next few months the question would return: "What kind of exercises are you going to give them?" Finally I started devising exercises. I was already perfectly aware that thinking of the world as a huge clockwork mechanism was a big mistake of Western civilization and the source of many of our troubles. My Eco-philosophy taught me that we must look at the world quite differently, namely as a sanctuary. If the world is a sanctuary, then the most appropriate mode of our behaviour in the world so conceived is *reverence*. Thus, we must practice reverence as a right mode of our being in the world.

Within a year the first principles (and respective practices) had articulated themselves. A year or so later, other principles fell into place. These principles and practices I then shared with my students in my workshops, especially in Theologos, Greece. The reception was good. I knew I was on the right track. Finally I published the book entitled : *Eco-Yoga, Practice and Meditations for Walking in Beauty on the Earth,* Gaia Books, London, 1994.

One of the main emphases is of Eco-Yoga is on *Empathy* : empathy with nature and all its elements; empathy with the rock and the brook and the tree - so that we return to our cosmic origins. We are estranged and alienated from ourselves because we are estranged and alienated from living nature and the living cosmos.

Thus, go to this rock and embrace it, become it... fully merge with it, until you remember, in your cosmic memory, what it 'felt' like to be a rock. Go to this tree and embrace it; become it; relive your past as a tree. The result of these yogic exercises is cleansing the system and going back to your origins. Empathy is one of the six major exercises of Eco-Yoga. The short presentation of the ideas and practices of Eco-Yoga contained in this essay gives the reader only a glimpse. A more systematic treatment can be found in my book on the subject.

What is the main reason for introducing Eco-Yoga? It is simple. You cannot live in peace if the whole world around you is at war with nature and destroying it. Making peace with nature and healing nature, establishing the balance and harmony with nature and all its creatures is a necessary part of your inner peace. I cannot emphasize strongly enough that once you understand the interconnectedness of all the elements of nature; once you understand the suffering of nature being the result of many broken and mutilated cycles; once you understand that you and nature are one; that we are all one; once you understand all that, you are bound to take the responsibility for the well being of the entire world. Your inner harmony must be extended to include the harmony in the outside world.

In order to establish this large harmony, the traditional yoga are clearly insufficient. They are limited to the individual and his/her individual universe. Hence the importance and necessity of Eco-Yoga. Eco-Yoga does not eliminate or replace traditional yoga. It amplifies their scope and supplements them with the exercises and concerns which are truly necessary for establishing lasting inner peace, a peace that embraces other humans and the world at large. What is specific and unique about Eco-Yoga?

1. It emphasizes the importance of being at one with nature and with the whole cosmos. Moreover, it provides specific exercises for re-weaving ourselves into the tapestry of the cosmos while we are healing ourselves. To be friends with the cosmos is a beautiful thing in itself. But also a precondition of being a true friend of yourself. As the scope of your love grows, so you grow.

2. It emphasizes the importance of the exercises of empathy and of reverence - for the elements and the entire nature, through which we come to view the whole world reverentially; we come to view other people reverentially; we come to treat ourselves reverentially; so that in the long run we dwell in a reverential world, within which it is much more easy to establish inner peace than in the world torn by conflicts, antagonism, animosity and irreverence.

3. It emphasizes the importance of responsibility for your own life, for the life of future generations, for all there is. To exercise one's responsibility in a beautiful manner is empowering and inspiring to others. It is a form of yoga, is an essential part of Eco-Yoga.

4. It emphasizes the importance of self empowerment. Eco-Yoga is ultimately about empowerment : so that you are empowered to establish your inner peace, so that you are empowered to help others and future generations, so that you are empowered to heal nature - without which your inner peace will be incomplete.

5. It emphasizes that time is your friend. Yes, time is your friend. Repeat this to yourself often : "Time is my friend." Once you befriend time, time will become a friend to you. And all other tasks will be so much more manageable.

In brief, Eco-Yoga is a path of beauty and sanity for our times.

Eco-Yoga as a Spiritual Exercise

All traditional and present forms of yoga are missing something which is very important in their search for wholeness and harmony. This statement doesn't deny that most systems of yoga offer us profound insights and illuminating exercises concerning our inner peace and well being.

What is missing in these traditional systems is the perception of the enormity of the ecological crisis and the consequences of this crisis on our individual life styles and on our relationships with the world and with the divine. These consequences are so far reaching and so important that their full understanding requires and necessitates reorienting the traditional spiritual practices, including yoga practices, so that their active pursuit truly leads to wholeness and harmony which are relevant to our present world. Right understanding of ecological action which also means right understanding of our responsibility towards the present world leads to such a conception of spiritual life in which Eco-yoga is a spiritual exercise, and not only a spade work towards the preservation of natural resources.

Let me share with you a personal experience which illustrates my point. Upon my arrival at Adyar, near Chennai (Madras), I found the beach terribly dirty, full of plastics and other debris - the result of recent and unusually strong storms. One of my beloved beaches has become an eyesore. What to do? One solution is not to go to the beach any more - a form of escapism and hiding. The other solution is somehow to ignore the mess and concentrate on the thin sliver of clean sand and the eternal waves and their continuous mesmerizing rhythm, expressing one of the great glories of nature. If you don't like something around you, ignore it. A seemingly rational strategy. But not quite so. For it leads to numbing your sensitivities. It leads to the acceptance of ugliness and pollution as a normal state of life. Deeper down, it leads to the renunciation of the quest for beauty and also of the sense of responsibility.

Beauty is essential to human life - whether we are aware of this or not. When we are deprived of it, we wither inwardly. When our senses are violated by ugly and polluted environment, our soul is bruised and it suffers.

When we relinquish our responsibility for making our life beautiful, and if possible holy, when we agree to tolerate ugly and filthy environment (because it is not our business to do anything about it) we somehow undermine our own dignity, the sense that life is precious, that we live in the world which is a sanctuary and we ourselves are a sanctuary. This again hurts our soul and undermines our spiritual well being. Thus you cannot tolerate ugliness around you without suffering some detrimental consequences.

So what have I done with the beach? I decided to clean it - with a large group of people, the scouts, the scholars, the students. To clean it not because it was just a dirty beach. But to clean it because we did not want to acknowledge another retreat, another pain of something beautiful turned into something ugly, which was going to seep its poison into our hearts and souls.

Cleaning the beach is a metaphor for our ecological responsibility and our inner cleansing. We can live with the environmental squalor. We can rationalize: we have not made it. So why should we bother? Yes, we can train our perception and somehow not see the pollution around us. We can develop the attitude of unseeing and cultivate a sort of amnesia for all environmental debacles. We can do that. But a price. The price is numbing our sensitivities, impairing our souls and dooming ourselves to a spiritual ghetto. When we are in this condition, other spiritual exercises and forms of yoga, which purportedly bring us into total harmony and wholeness, are a bit of pretence, and perhaps even lead to a self-delusion of perfection. For how can we pretend to be in full harmony with ourselves while our brothers and sisters in nature cry for help, while Mother Earth is crying for help and bleeding, while we ourselves (the whole human race) are at war with nature?

Eco-Yoga is precisely this form of perception and this form of practice which brings us to a spiritual alignment in our present world - full of new agonies, crises and dilemmas. This alignment not only means understanding new suffering and agonies, unprecedented in history as we ourselves, for instance, are ridden with invisible chemical and environmental bullets. It also outlines new imperatives for action : ethical, spiritual and practical so that we do not only talk abstractly of harmony and wholeness but try to bring it about in our reality. Our present problems are quite new. The old yoga and older teachings never envisaged them. Hence the necessity of new perceptions and new yoga, one of which is Eco-Yoga. We have to engage in Eco-yoga for yet another reason - in order not to leave bad ecological Karma behind us.

Here then is the summary of Eco-Yoga as a spiritual practice.

- We clean the environment not to dirty our hands but in order to clean our souls.
- Beauty is essential for human life. When our environment is uglified and debased, we suffer a slow psychic death.
- Peace with nature is a precondition of our inner peace. To make peace with nature we have to mend our ways. We have to let nature breathe by removing from it most foul pollutants. This is also the way to our improved physical and mental health. The everlasting sense of inner harmony and union, which all yogas postulate, cannot be achieved unless we fully understand how vital our peace with nature is; and unless we act on this understanding. You cannot truly reach for God or for the divine if you allow yourself to live in squalor, in inner mess and filth.
- The beach, of which we have spoken, is really a symbol. It relates to your courtyard; and the world outside which is a part of your outer skin. You have to care for it because it is part of your responsibility for your inner beauty. We clean the beach because we are beautiful beings striving for beauty and becoming it.
- The ecologists and eco-philosophers are not tedious fellows who revel in frightening people with ozone holes, stories of environmental horrors, and civilization's diseases. We are modern days Rishis who search and meditate on what is required for a true balance, wholeness, harmony, and peace.

Mahayoga

We may now introduce the concept of Mahayoga. As we

go through life, we have so many choices to make. As we have complicated our lives in the technological society, we have more choices to make. Often we feel, we have too many choices to make, and not infrequently we are at a loss. Thus we have to have some inner guidance. We must make choices which strike right balances. We must make choices which lead to important balances.

Mahayoga informs us that the overall balance and harmony signifies the balance within our bodies, but also the balance in our hearts and souls; but also the balance and harmony with other beings in the world. Striving for justice to enable others to live, striving for the harmony with nature is a necessary part of Mahayoga. Otherwise our yoga will be too puny, too partial, establishing illusory balances and harmonies.

The practice of Mahayoga comes from our deeper understanding of our responsibilities in this truly magnificent and yet so intricately connected world in which *we have to take care of the entire web of life.* Otherwise you may be striking limited balances in your corner of the web of life at the expense of other parts of the web. Mahayoga is the yoga for the entire web of life.

Mahayoga is not practiced as the result of your pity for poor people and over-exploited nature. It is practiced for your spiritual balance, as you genuinely see that you are one with the universe, that all beings are your relations, that true compassion means the yoga of life which embraces all.

Mahayoga contains all other yogas. It comprises the yoga of empowerment and the yoga of wisdom, which we shall discuss next. It contains the yoga of the Himalayan wonder as well as outlines the path of ethics and the path of right politics; it provides the key to happiness and it spells out the importance of vision.

Mahayoga is the yoga of life that embraces all-the whole world, the whole web of life. To practice Mahayoga aright is to remember that we always are a part of the web of life, its pulsating rhythm, and its unique and extraordinary wholeness.

Chapter 4

The Yoga of Empowerment

The Energy Addiction

We are a very powerful civilization. Yet as individuals we are weak and disempowered. We need to ask the question: Why amidst this abundance of power we, as individuals, feel so powerless? We need to understand this problem in order to understand deeper the nature of our civilization. But also for a practical reason. We want to practice our yogas to some effect. We want to live a life of dignity. Therefore we must not allow the paralyzing forces, unleashed by strange mechanisms of history, to incapacitate and paralyze us. The yoga of empowerment is a strategy which enables us to safeguard the paths to other yogas, to remove the rubble and obstacles from our ways, to keep away the poisons of various kinds from our system. Since those impediments are so numerous and often so insidious - so much so that life can be considered to be an obstacle course - we need some strategies and technics to combat them. These strategies and technics make the yoga of empowerment.

Ivan Illich, one of the most perceptive critics of the pitfalls of our civilization, wrote a little book entitled *Energy and Equity,* (1974). In it he demonstrated that using too much energy per capita may not be too good for us. Up to certain point, the increased use of energy contributes to our individual well being and to social cohesion and equity. *Beyond* this point the story is different. We become energy gluttons. We become energy addicts. We become so dependent on energy that gradually we lose our independence. How can that be?

The more energy we use, the more gadgets we use. The more gadgets we use, the less self-reliant we become. Our gadgets become our crutches. Technological civilization encourages an extreme specialization. There is a gadget for every simple function we want to perform. And there are specialists for various gadgets. We are encouraged to think that beyond our narrow expertise, we are incompetent to do anything. Thus an excessive reliance on gadgets, combined with an excessive drive towards specialization disengages us from life, and gradually disempowers us.

However, Life is wonderfully versatile and extremely competent in doing everything for itself. We are this life itself. We are equipped by nature to do so many things. When we are in the garden, we thrive because we do so many things. And we don't want anybody to bring to us a machine for tying tomato plants to the sticks.

Thus one of the important sources of disempowerment, in present times, is our mute agreement to allow gadgets to run our lives. The result is diminishing our self-reliance and our responsibility. The more you delegate to gadgets, machines, and energy slaves, the less you become a person. What can you do? Slowly try to regain you sovereignty and self-reliance. How? By various means. Don't allow yourself to be persuaded that you are incapable, and that everything must be done for you by specialists. Try to use simple gadgets. Better still, try not to use them unless you must. Try not to use your car — unless necessary. Walking is so good for you, for your health, for the moments of meditation in which you may engage when you pass a lovely flower. Using simple things over which you have control is empowering. Not using countless devices, which actually clutter your life, is empowering. Walking and biking whenever you can is empowering. Making you life simpler is empowering.

The Idols of the Marketplace

Francis Bacon (1561-1626) was already, in the 17th Century, much alarmed that our minds are so manipulated by current opinions and dogmas. He distinguished four main idols of the marketplace - which muzzle our intellect and attempt to subjugate our freedom of thought to the demands of authority, of prejudice, of the status quo, of those who want to control us.

Now in our times the power of the idols of the marketplace is not diminished but increased. And this power is more manipulative and more insidious. The master idol is of course the television. Its influence is so enormous. We seem to be helpless to do anything about it. We do not need the myth of Leviathan who devours his own children. Television is the Leviathan of our times. Oh, do not tell me what television could have become, if... I am talking about TV as it has been. Its influence is particularly crippling in the United States, when, on average, children from the ages of 5 to 18 spend more hours in front of the telly than in the classroom. Thinking people and the authorities are alarmed in the United States by the decline of the level of education in America. Well, television is one of the causes.

So what do you do personally about TV and other mass media which diligently work on you — as a prospective consumer and a cipher which can be manipulated and persuaded? Let us acknowledge that if you live in this world, among people, you cannot avoid being influenced. You always are and want to be. The question is: By whom are you being influenced? By Mahatma Gandhi or by a slippery fellow who wants to sell you an electric toothbrush, fattening puddings, or a new car? Remember: As we are influenced, so we build our karma. Let us remember with T.S. Eliot:

> Of what you have done in the past
> You eat the fruit
> Either rotten or ripe.

Let us again look at a larger picture. We are not snipping at television simply because we do not like the strategy of hard sale. We are objecting on a much more fundamental level. The purpose of yoga is to infuse meaning and dignity into your life. To live meaningfully in this day and age, we need to do so much healing of ourselves and of the planet. Empowerment (in our times) is a form of responsibility which we take for the life of the planet and for our own lives. We object against the institution of TV and its influence because instead of helping us to heal the earth, it encourages us to devastate it further. Instead of helping us to lead connected lives, it does the opposite — by reducing us to the miasma of fears and insecurities. If the forces undercutting the elan of life itself are to be called evil, then TV (in our times) is evil. Let us have the courage of our judgement. Let us not be confused with the plethora of ambiguities and half-truths. Television of our times does not serve human purposes, does not serve the purposes of empowering us.

Yes, in seeking your paths of empowerment you need to be clear about the nature of good and evil. We are not going to preach here any fundamentalist morality. Our mission is simple. We want to regain our meaning and dignity. For this reason we cannot be tolerant about everything. We cannot agree that anything goes. For if anything goes, hard drugs are permitted, the destruction of the earth is permitted, the manipulation of your mind and your freedom is permitted — and then if this process goes on, we go down the tube of history as mute ciphers.

But no. We make our stand — which is one for the sanctity of life, for reverence of all life. Our basic moral premise is that what is life-enhancing in the long run, is good. What undercuts the vital roots of life, is evil. We are aware that sometimes making decisions and judgements on these matters is difficult. But we have a clear perspective what is good for all life in the long run. We have a clear awareness what is healing and what is wounding. Let us rely on these intuitions and perceptions. Let us not allow the idols of the marketplace to blind us. Let us practice the yoga of life by our fierce allegience to the beauty of life. One of the principles of the yoga of empowerment is to accept that you are a guardian of life itself.

Arete The ancient Greeks were a remarkable people. They introduced to the world democracy and philosophy, unforgettable tragedies and unsurpassed sculptors. But they were also artists of life. They knew how to live — in joy and with depth. They were aware of the divinity of the universe. But also of the god-within, which lies dormant within us and which requires a real effort to be brought out to shine through.

Although they did not use the term yoga, they evolved distinctive strategies of life for which the term yoga would be quite appropriate. In addition to specific technics (of wine making and pottery making) and concepts (used in philosophy and public life) they valued overall *organizing principles*. One of them was the notion of *harmony*, which they saw as underlying all the universe, all art, all human endeavours. To be accomplished and wise was to understand this overall harmony, was to weave yourself into its patterns, was to conduct your life and thought in a harmonious way, in congruence with the underlying laws of harmony, for only then would your life and work possess truth, goodness, and quality. This principle of harmony was an immensely powerful guiding force which enabled them to see things wholistically and to see their lives (and health) as related to the overall harmony of the cosmos. Why did I mention health? Because health too was seen as a matter of harmony within the body, and of the body with all the other energies of the universe. Thus Plato defines health as a consummated love affair of the organs of the body. It is quite lovely, isn't it? It required an all embracing mind to see health in this perspective. The perspective of the mind is important, for it provides the guiding principles which make things coherent, lucid and harmonious.

Another organizing principle of the universe of the ancient Greeks was arete — conceived as striving for perfection, for excellence, for ultimate limits of the human achievement. Arete was not a technical concept aiming to achieve the greatest dexterity within a given field or craft. The so-called "quest for excellence" which became trendy in American industry in the late 1980's is a limited idea. It focuses on efficiency, precision, competition. In the competitive modern industry, you try to reach excellence in order to prevail over your competitors. With the Greeks, you tried to achieve perfection, arete, in order to express the everlasting harmony.

We should be perfectly aware that arete was connected with harmony. In order to come close to the laws underlying harmony, in order to express this harmony through human artifacts, you require a superhuman effort. Hence arete — striving to reach the limits of human perfectability. Thus arete was an expression of beauty, of goodness, of integrity, of quality (of which Robert Pirsig speaks so much in his book, *Zen and the Art of Motorcycle Maintenance)*.

The Greeks took the idea of arete with great seriousness and verve. In field after field, they excelled. While reaching the human limits in arts, they stretched and extended themselves. The *Greek way of life was the practice* of the yoga of arete. This is the foundation of the greatness of the Greek culture.

The practice of arete is a practice of the yoga of empowerment. By continually practising arete, the Greeks of the Golden Era particularly kept empowering themselves. And by Zeus, they were empowered people!

In brief, the practice of arete is an important aspect of the yoga of empowerment — in all times and in every society. Doing things well, doing things with quality is empowering — even if these are small things of daily life. People who do things well continually re-empower themselves. It is important for each of us to do at least certain things well.

Without wishing to belabor the point, we need to reflect a little deeper (while we hold the idea of arete as the background) that our very powerful civilization produces so many disempowered people. Why? Because the present economic system called the Free Market :

— thrives on failure, and haunts everybody by the idea of failure;
— makes a real achievement nearly impossible, for "success" means climbing the ladder that never ends (often climbing on the backs of others);
— bars us from the practice of arete. Through homogenizing the world it reduces us to repetitive ciphers, and enslaves us to the machine (even if it is a sophisticated computer), instead of inspiring us to pursue beauty, integrity, and quality.

Artisans, craftsmen and people shaping things with their hands are fortunate. They have the opportunity to empower themselves as they shape things through their own will and imagination. Doing things with hands and with your own body is not only a biological necessity. It is also a form of empowerment. We always revive when we have the opportunity to fashion things creatively, to give them a bit of our soul, to express through them our energies, dreams and aspirations. For what is empowerment if not infusing part of your spirit into things of general significance so that your spirit breathes with the Great Spirit of all things?

Now we need to practise arete, and not only talk about it. It is empowering to know how empowering the practice of arete is. You need to outline some activities in which you are good, and you need to practice them in the spirit of arete. But practice you must — not only make a determination that you will practice them. Doing things well is important and empowering. To do daily meditation systematically is empowering. To prepare your favorite dish well, while you enjoy doing it, is empowering.

Positive Strategies of Empowerment

Among specific technics and strategies of empowerment are :

I. Imitation

II. Visualization

III. Turning Adversity into Advantage

IV. Beholding Positive Ideas

V. Participation

Let us look into those strategies in some depth.

Imitation :- Imitation is the most ancient of the arts of empowerment. It predates the humans. When small birds begin to fly, they imitate their parents. When lion cubs begin to hunt, they imitate their elders. When finally small children learn to talk, they have a delicious tendency to repeat a new word over and over with a great delight. That is how they empower themselves to speak freely later. Those basic skills must be learnt at appropriate times. If for some reasons the right period is missed, and the language, for instance, is not acquired at the proper age, the individual has great difficulties in coping with life. The stories of wolf-children demonstrated this amply. Thus, the strategy of imitation is to trigger the basic skills which are latent in us all.

Yet imitation has many other important aspects. We go through life acquiring various kinds of skills — from very rudimentary to very refined. Let us visit the work place of a Renaissance painter. There are all kinds of young people there. Some are mixing paints, some are varnishing the frames and some are helping the master to execute the masterpieces. They learn not only how to put the paint on the canvas but also how to express the depth of human eyes in the master's tradition. They learn through osmosis, through trying over and again to capture the incredible subtle aspects of the human face.

A similar process is going on when you learn to play music from great masters. You can not learn by reading how to play music. You cannot even learn from listening to good music. You learn by being with masters, seeing and repeating how they do it, being guided by them, acquiring this particular quality of sounds; learning how phrases are expressed and how to put together the architecture of the whole thing. So much of our refined skills and high knowledge is learning from the masters, looking up to the masters and trying to match them. If we can do that, then we are on the road to arete. Thus the second important strategy of imitation, as part of empowerment, is taking a clue from the masters.

Let us go to another important realm. For a number of years the North Wall of Eiger, in the Alps, was deemed unconquerable. Every expedition of the most accomplished Alpinists which attempted to scale this wall failed. The climbers never returned as they were frozen somewhere in the middle of this magnificent monster. Then in 1934 yet another expedition of two climbers went. This time they scaled it through. From this moment on the myth of the unconquerability of Eiger vanished. Every next expedition just climbed it through without much problem — no doubt empowered by the first ascent. The inspiring thing for those who followed the first team was: if they could do it, so can we. Here imitation means repeating the achievement of others by extending your own limits.

It is a great motivating force to know that a thing can be done, and was already done. This psychological factor is very important. What is at one point considered impossible, and paralyzing at the very thought of trying, becomes an invitation to an adventure. In the third sense, empowering through imitation is extending your own limits to the highest achieved, is stretching yourself beyond the hum-drum and ordinary.

Imitation is also important in spiritual life. We all have heard about the book *The Imitation of Christ by* Thomas a Kempis. The title encapsulates the whole idea. Monks and nuns, and lay religious people, so often derive their energy and sustenance by following the example of an illustrious one, be it Christ, the Buddha, or Zarathustra. The spiritual power of a great example is second to none. Following an example of a great one is empowering. For again we are persuaded that this celestial path is possible. This time we do not climb the North Wall of Eiger. But negotiate much subtler terrain of spiritual peaks and valleys. In the fourth sense, the imitation of saints and illustrious beings is empowering ourselves in the process of actualization of our spiritual potential.

Imitation is (in summary) the capacity to repeat well what others have done, is the capacity to claim as your own some of the skills of human kind. Imitation is the prowess and pride to join the ranks of those who have excelled. Imitation is not aping things mindlessly but meshing the skills developed by evolution and proudly claiming them as your own.

Visualization :- Visualization is a powerful mind-technic which is used is rarely. Visualization is a form of day dreaming which — through a strange alchemy that occurs between mind and reality — can transform mind-states into reality. How this happens we do not know. It is a bit of a mystery. There are many important things that we do not know. We do not know what energy is and how it is transformed into work. We do not know what the atom is or the electron, etc. We should cherish and celebrate mystery, rather than be afraid of it. Albert Einstein so speaks of mystery:

"The most beautiful thing we can experience is the mysterious. It is the source of all true art and science. He to whom this emotion is a stranger, who can no longer pause to wonder and stand wrapped in awe, is as good as dead: His eyes are closed."

The power of visualization actually is the power of the mind. Mind is partaking in everything we do in a much larger degree than we are aware of. Let us look at therapy. It has been found and affirmed that visualization may be very significant factor in combatting cancer. The patient is required to imagine, literally to visualize, his blood cells eating cancer cells. In many cases this process, when performed with great application and determination, has led to remarkable results. But you must not be lukewarm about it. You must visualize things with power and intensity. You must actually eat cancer cells with your mind. Only then does visualization work at its best.

Of late we have witnessed the emergence of a new medical field: Psycho-neuro-immunology. This is precisely the field which recognizes and tries to explain in scientific terms how the states of our mind can influence and alter the states of our body, including the chemistry of our body processes.

How can you use visualization in your daily life? One strategy is to imagine, in concrete palpable terms, the positive outcome of what you want to accomplish. You see it so very clearly — in your mind. It is there. Done. Let us then take those necessary steps in reality to bring your vision to fruition. Be aware, you have to have courage, and determination to imagine, to visualize the positive outcome — as well as the steps leading to it. Be also aware that visualization may be disempowering when you are gripped by fear, negative feelings, uncertainty, weakness of the heart. Then you start imagining that you cannot succeed, that you must fail; you actually see yourself as having failed. Then you do not help yourself; you actually hinder yourself by bringing through visualization the negative outcome of your activity. The stuff of mind is a very subtle thing.

Surely (some may respond) you cannot always charge in this positive mood while there are so often risks involved and the possibility of failure is around the corner. Yes, you can always be positive. There are risks involved. And you may not succeed. But you must create in your mind the best positive scenario to help yourself to succeed.

Another powerful application of visualization is in creating the kind of person you want to be. Ask yourself: What kind of person do I want to be? Then imagine (visualize!) what you look like, behave like, think like when you are this person. Study this person well. Then act out this person in real life. And watch it all the time — what you should be feeling, doing and saying, if you were that person. In a sense you are now performing the strategy of imitation: You are imitating this person which you have projected yourself to become. A very subtle strategy.

As we said, the reality of mind is subtle. Therefore we have to use the power of visualization with caution. Actually, there are so many forms of visualization. If you are not familiar with those technics of the mind, the best thing is to take one or two workshops on guided imaginary journeys. And then go on your own journeys.

Visualization is, in brief, empowering yourself by calling on your inner powers which you have within you, and which are ready to help you if you are in need; and if you treat them well. You need to be friendly with those forces. They are a part of you. But pay attention! Pay attention to your inner self.

Turning Adversity into Advantage :- We try to plan our lives with care, if not with prudence. Then unexpectedly, due to some events in the outside world, or because of our own slips (often a combination of the two) things fall apart. We feel overrun, undone, helpless, and disempowered. This has happened to everybody.

I was about to return to Poland from the island of Thassos at the beginning of September, 1992. I was convinced my plane from Kavala (near Thassos) to Athens was on Wednesday night; the flight to Warsaw was to follow a few hours later. I was in good shape during the entire day on Tuesday. All packing was done. There was enough time to go to the fields to pick up walnuts from the trees and fresh figs — in abundance at this time. All was well.

Except that not all is well. Around 7 pm, I decided to re-check the dates of my departure. I looked at the ticket, I looked at my diary — and my heart sunk. Oh no! My plane to Athens was to leave tonight, in one hour. My sense of well being disappeared completely. I had the feeling of total dejection. So stupid — not to have rechecked the dates a few days earlier, or at least in the morning. How can you do such a thing? How can you? !

So I admonished myself over and again. There was no way I could catch the plane in one hour. It takes an hour from the village to the ferry. Then another forty-five minutes on the ferry. Then a half-hour by taxi to the airport. I was done in. Or rather, undone. I would miss my plane to Warsaw, too. Two conferences were awaiting me in Poland the day after. As usual, I had restricted tickets that did not allow for any changes. What a mess!

But remember, the mess is always within you. If you allow it to dominate you, it will roll over you, and make you feel miserable, inadequate, helpless, disempowered. Thus I had to shake off this feeling of despondency. I went to the garden. The sun was setting. I breathed deeply. I told myself that it is just one of these things. My misery would not help the matter.

Then I went to the best taverna of the village with a French friend. Dining on the terrace, to the accompaniment of the crickets and the local wine helped. Next day, I deliberately put myself in a relaxed, spacious frame of mind. While in Athens I checked into a really good hotel, usually too expensive for my purse. You see, in such circumstances, you need to treat yourself well. There is some healing and mending inside to be done. A bit of compassion for yourself and pampering is justifiable, and recommended. In the evening I went to the Plaka, a section of Athens just below the Acropolis, always vivacious and lively. I had a wonderful, peaceful night at the Electra Palace Hotel. Next morning I started the day in a very positive mood. At this point I was beginning to turn the adversity into advantage.

After breakfast I went to straighten my ticket to Warsaw. It wasn't as bad as my worst scenario had anticipated. Spaces were available and I didn't have to buy a new ticket. In most trying circumstances, the situation is never as bad as our gloomiest anticpations envision.

In the afternoon I really used my time with God's blessing. I went to the ancient Agora of Athens for a long meditation. I had the whole afternoon given to me! I submerged myself in the spirit of the Agora. I imagined Socrates, Pericles, and Alcybiades walking around me. I saw in my mind's eyes the sculptor Phidias directing the work on the Acropolis; and I saw the countless craftsmen carrying out the monumental work on the Acropolis. After all, I was in the city of cities, from which everything of greatness has sprung — like Athena from Zeus's head. It was thrilling and elevating to have those five hours among those noble stones, where great spirits walked around. I asked myself whether I didn't make this "mistake" deliberately (although sub-consciously) in order to have this spiritual feast. I now turned my adversity into advantage. I knew that what would stay in my memory of those two days in Athens would be this glorious meditation at the Agora.

Beholding Positive Ideas :- In addition to specific technics, there are some large ideas which are pregnant with positive energy. To behold these ideas, to make them a part of our universe, is empowering.

Hope is empowering. When hope dwindles, empowerment is undermined. Hope is the condition of any empowerment. Hopelessness is disempowerment.

Right Cosmology is empowerment. Conceiving the world as a sanctuary is empowering. Conceiving the world as a machine is disempowering. May be here lies part of our trouble — a wrong cosmology that has disempowered the whole civilization.

The sense of confidence (I can do it!) is empowering.

Striving for arete is empowering.

The sense of your own self worth (I am a shining particle of the Great Cosmos) is empowering.

Walking in beauty is empowering.

Wisdom is empowering. Let us remember that wisdom is more than information.

> "Where is the wisdom we have lost in knowledge?
>
> Where is the knowledge we have lost in information?"
>
> — T.S.Eliot

Prayer can be empowering, but not one in which you ask God to give you this or that, but one in which you raise yourself to the level of divinity and converse with God about important matters.

Responsibility (I am responsible) is empowering.

Enlightenment is empowering. Who is enlightened is empowered.

Joy is empowering. Oh what a joy to walk peacefully through life, while beholding joy as a natural condition of living!

Love is empowering. Lovers of the cosmos know it. It is a blessed condition to be able to love. It is a privileged condition to be loved.

The accumulation of positive karma is one of the most important sources of empowerment. If you continue to live in harmony, this harmony works for you. Thus, to treat yourself with reverence, to treat other humans with reverence, to treat the entire cosmos with reverence, is empowering.

Participation :- Whatever we do in this world, we participate. Even if we do nothing, our body participates in countless cycles, and our mind is ticking away connecting us with so many things. The whole universe is one stupendous participatory process.

Participation is one of the primary modes of acquiring empowerment. When growing boys joined a group of hunters in old societies, this was for them a form of empowerment.

When young people in our times participate in social games or in dancing together, they develop their social skills and confidence. They get empowered. Participation is so important in our lives and so common that we forget how important it is. We take it for granted and neglect to develop its latent powers.

Yet there are forms and forms of participation. Playing with other people the game called "Trivial Pursuit" is a form of participation. But, as its name properly says, it is a trivial participation. Choosing a box of detergent among twenty different brands, or choosing a box of corn flakes among fifteen different kinds is exercising your choice, is a form of participation. However, do not think that you can participate in too many trivial games and activities without being trivialized in the end. Why has our present civilization so trivialized our lives? Because we have allowed ourselves to be sucked into too many trivial forms of activities; put otherwise, because we don't have enough discernment and wisdom.

How do you distinguish between trivial and significant forms of participation? Often you know it intuitively, if you just reflect a little. On a deeper level of analysis, trivial participation is one that bores you, leaves behind a sense of shallowness, contributes little to your deeper sense of life. Significant participation, on the other hand, engages you and sometimes enthralls you, leaves behind a sense of satisfaction, contributes to the meaning of your life.

Nearly all forms of participation occur in some kind of context, which is governed by some kinds of rules. We usually are aware of the rules of the game (be it tennis, basketball, bridge, or chess) and we participate in the game because in spite of the rules we can exert our prowess, show our intelligence, manifest something of our being.

Unsatisfactory forms of participation are those which, in addition to explicit rules, are controlled by hidden rules which are manipulated by others. We are frustrated in such circumstances because we are led to believe that we participate, while it is a pseudo-participation. We are puppets on some stage while others are pulling the strings. If we are controlled and manipulated, life in us is thwarted. It is as simple as that. True participation is a manifestation of the exuberance of life. There is no exuberance of life in playing "Trivial Pursuit", in choosing a box of corn flakes in the supermarket, in voting in an election completely controlled by the hidden players.

Thus significant participation requires your active partaking, requires being creative. If you are creative, in any field or endeavour, especially the arts, you exert your intelligence and ultimately involve your soul. Truly creative participation is singing with the universe. All transformations in the universe have occurred as the result of creative participation.

Now, let us be mindful about the context. The deeper and more significant the context, the more significant the form of participation. The shallower the context the shallower the participation — the shallower your life.

"He who thinks of God becomes God." This is not a blasphemy but identifying a very deep spiritual context: If you constantly contemplate the divine aspects and attributes of the world and try to make your life congruent with these attributes, you are on the way to divinity. Remember, karma is all pervading. As you think so you become. As you participate so you carve your destiny — in the image of trivial pursuits or in the image of the illustrious ones.

All the strategies of self-empowerment should not be considered as independent process of separate muscle building, but one process of tuning up the entire field of your life-energy. A difficult task? Maybe. But what else is there to life? Participating in trivial pursuits? We have had enough of that! Let us therefore embark on those journeys in which creative participation is of the essence. Authentic life is an empowered life. Let us empower ourselves: this is the condition of living in meaning and with dignity.

Chapter 5

The Yoga of Wisdom

The Himalayan Journey

We don't exactly know what wisdom is. But we all want to acquire it. The history of humanity is the history of our struggle against our unwisdom. This is what all sacred texts tell us.

Some sages and prophets have insisted that each of us is perfect—as we are at this very moment. This is an over optimistic view and a dangerous one, encouraging people to think that the spiritual journey is easy and that salvation is of hand. Alas, this is not true.

This potential divinity, which resides in each of us, is a wonderful gift of heaven. But to actualize it is an arduous and demanding task, which requires extraordinary will-power stamina, resilience and perseverence. For this reason, although many are called only very few are chosen.

How do we learn to write? First we learn the alphabet. Then single words. Then simple sentences. Then we learn to write a narrative. And finally, we write poetry. Poetry comes at the end of the process, not at the beginning. And so it is with spiritual perfection. It comes at the end of a long journey.

He who insists that it is an easy quest is not quite responsible, or simply does not understand the nature of things.

At the end of this exquisite process which is called the spiritual becoming all is clear, translucent and effortless. But the process of ascending itself is another matter. It is full of hardships, dangerous crevices and slippery slopes. Whoever is acquainted with the nature of Himalayan climbing, understands well that it is a most demanding and taxing enterprise. And so is the spiritual ascent. And even more so. The spiritual quest is truly a Himalayan journey.

To arrive at the steps of wisdom, one has to have the experience of real life. One needs to submerge oneself in it, and suffer with it. Even Lord Buddha had to go through suffering before reaching wisdom and enlightenment. We cannot reach wisdom while being isolated from life. We cannot acquire wisdom by steeping ourselves in wisdom only. Wisdom is of the world and for the world . Wisdom and Dharma serve the world and all its beings.

The Invisible Sources of Sustenance

We strive for wisdom in order to arrive at a deeper life. Ordinary knowledge focuses on so called good life, which means materially satisfactory life. The focus of wisdom is different. Now while saying that we strive for a deeper life, we are not renouncing good life. We are rather emphasizing that we are aiming at a better life. For deeper life is a better life.

Wisdom is not only the state of our mind. It is the state of our entire being. It is such a subtle affair that one hesitates to assert with certainty whether it can be taught or learnt. Yet, it can be acquired because nobody is born wise. Therefore in some way it is learnt, and in some way it is taught. But these ways are subtle.

There are many steps and strategies outlining the almost invisible path of wisdom. Some of these are discursive and clear, almost compelling to reason. Some others are not so obvious, as they require a recourse to intuition, to meditation and to deeper reflection on the nature of things and on the nature of the self. To begin with, there are some preliminaries which are necessary in order to pursue higher paths of wisdom. Among these preliminaries is the acquisition of a larger sense of oneself, which means articulating within ourselves these dimensions of our being which are carriers and vehicles of wisdom. These dimensions or qualities cannot be learnt through and via scientific knowledge because they are not there. They have to be acquired through our uniquely human journey.

Dimensions of our enlarged self:

1. Discernment
2. Judgement
3. Distance
4. Compassion
5. Holistic sense of the universe
6. Hope
7. Courage

We shall discuss them one by one.

Discernment is the faculty which informs us what counts and why.

It is this beam of laser light, from within, which goes beyond the surface of facts to reveal the deeper nature of things. One pound of clay and one pound of gold are just two lumps of matter. Scientific reason cannot inform us which is more valuable. It is quite logical to argue that clay is more useful because we can fix with it the holes in our houses. But this is not how we view the situation in the world at large. Discernment informs us about the value of gold vis-a-vis the value or clay. On another level discernment informs us about the value of love vis-a-vis material possessions, including gold. Through discernment we learn wisdom. And wisdom itself is a wonderful embodiment of discerment. To discern is divine. This is what great poets, artists and prophets possess–the power of discernment which enables them to see new light and then to create new worlds.

Judgement. is the capacity for weighing on the scales of one's soul what is important and why. We all remember the story of king Solomon and the two mothers, each claiming that the contested child was her own. Solomon declared. "Cut the child into two halves. Upon this verdict one mother immediately cried. "Oh no, give it to her." And Solomon ruled. "This is the true mother." No science can teach us this kind of judgement. Science quantifies. Judgement enshrines.

Judgement is a beautiful human faculty, profound in its nature and consequences. When misused it can lead to self-rightousness, which so often puts people down. When used wisely it is a jewel of a thing to possess. It is an invaluable guide, a supporter which gives us confidence in making decisions and in sailing through life with grace and dignity.

Judgement is an integral component of wisdom. Wisdom always judges and weighs things on its subtle scales—even when it insists that it is non-judgemental.

Discernment and judgement are the qualities which we develop from early childhood. But in the state of wisdom these qualities shine supreme. Without them our wisdom limps.

Sharp intellectual qualities, so much appreciated when we are doing mathematics and science, require different abilities than the ones exemplified by discernment and judgement, associated with wisdom.

Let me share with you a Sufi story. The Sufis were seekers of wisdom, a mystically oriented people, of the Islam faith. Many centuries ago, there were four young men searching for wisdom and magic. They read learned books and engaged in deep discussions. After some years they thought they were mature enough. They decided to test their wisdom in the world at large. From their little town—off they went to the world. They walked for many days. One day the three of them decided that they were the bright and clever ones. They refused to talk to the fourth one, who was less argumentative and talkative. But he kept walking with them. At one point he said to them. "You think that you are so superior. But I understand". They kept walking and refused to talk to the fourth one anyway.

Some days later they stumbled on a carcass of which only white bones were left. "This is carcass of a wild animal," said the first. "Oh yes, it is a carcass of a lion," said the second. The third said, "With my magic knowledge, I could re-animate it and bring it back to life." Then the fourth said, "Please don't do it because it will eat us all." But they did not listen, and started re-animating the carcass, while the fourth one ran to the tallest tree and climbed to the top of it.

Lo and behold, they brought the lion back to life. And very prompty he ate the three of them. After some time the lion went away. The fourth one slowly descended from the tree. Extremely sorry for his companions, he returned home.

Distance. Daily life is very rushed and immediate. It entangles us so closely that it does not leave enough space for reflection. We thus need to create distance from life and its hectic rhythm. We don't want to separate ourselves from life, but only to create this kind of space around ourselves which enables us to breathe more freely and to reflect on the meaning and vicissitudes of life more amply. This fastidious attitude of distance is a protective safety valve. But also a shawl of security. Distance and capacity to reflect are two sides of the same coin. You create distance not to be distant from life, but to lead a reflective life; better still, an examined life.

An aspect of the reflective life is the capacity for silence. Silence is your great ally. In silence we mature. In silence we reach our inner core. In silence we see things differently and even hear in new ways. Silence is the cradle of perfection. Silence is an indispensable companion for meditation, which is a gateway to enlightenment. The language of wisdom is the language of meaningful silence. The continuous chatter is the language of unwisdom. Cultivate silence for it cultivates you.

Compassion. As you enlarge your own domain you merge compassionetly with others. Compassion means to empathize with others so that you understand them deeper and better. By becoming them, you enlarge yourself and also understand yourself better. You are beginning to beat a common rhythm with the universe. What a joy to overcome the shell of your confinement !

Compassion is a form of empathy and universal sympathy towards all. But also a unique form of knowledge: you know them from within, which no objective knowledge can provide. With this knowledge from within your judgement of others is so much more subtle, refined and penetrating. Such a knowledge entails responsibility. Compassion in action means taking responsibility and care for others.

Making compassion an integral part of your lifestyle is an auspicious way to certify that you have entered a path of wisdom.

Thus you develop compassion to deepen your knowledge, understanding, insight; and also to enlarge the scope of your care and responsibility for others. Universal compassion, which is so much cherished among Buddhists, is a symbol of enlightenment. In this context a Buddha, Compassionate One, and a wise one are synonymous.

Holistic sense of the Universe. According to ancient fables, the hedgehog knows very many things but knows them superficially. The fox knows one big thing but well. We are a civilization of hedgehogs. We increasingly know more and more things. Alas, we know them more and more superficially.

This fragmented panorama of information, held in separate compartments of our brains, has undesirable consequences, both for our comprehension of knowledge and for the state of our being. We are unable to relate bits of knowledge from one department to fragments of knowledge in another department.

Knowledge does not integrate itself. It has to be integrated by exquisitely tuned minds. We do not possess such minds. We are the hedgehogs, accumulating bits of knowledge. Let us also clearly perceive that knowledge which we absorb is specialized in nature. Thus we are given specialized fragments not comprehensive wholes. So our hedgehog nature is only reinforced.

In the end we are as fragmented within as is our knowledge in our brains. It is all in pieces. All coherence gone. There is no centre that holds either in the scope of our knowledge or in the compass of our beings. Such a state of affairs was bound to profoundly influence the nature of our civilization, which is ridden by chaos, confusion, relativism and nihilism.

This state of things is antithetical to the nature of wisdom. Wisdom signifies coherence, holding onto the centre, discernment and judgement. Finally, wisdom signifies holism, a holistic vision of the world and of all there is. Let us notice that discernment and judgement are only possible if there is the centre which informs us how to judge; and what are the reasons for discernment.

Furthermore, the centre that holds is the invisible axis which coordinates all. It is around this invisible axis that things are woven, and by which they are assigned their place and their significance. When we speak of holism, we invariably imply a meaningful whole, made of parts which are coalescing together. What makes them coalesce and hold together is the centre that holds. When the centre is gone, coherence is gone.

We now understand why holism is so important. Searching for a holistic perspective is not a pipe dream but a necessary foundation for sane and coherent living. By bringing into the compass of wisdom its various components: discernment, judgement, coherence and the centre that holds, we are articulating life which is worth living.

There are many possible and desirable holistic perspectives. Each of us has to develop our own. A holistic perspective is nothing short of a philosophy. Before you accept and fully develop one, you have to be fastidious, discriminating, wise. Yes there is a problem here. To arrive at wisdom you have to possess a right holistic perspective. To build a right holism, you have to be wise.

We should be aware of two dangers. One is to accept too rashly a half-baked, superficial and shallow holism, which does not permit for a full articulation of your latent wisdom; and more important still, which is not deep enough to enable you to transcend wisdom, as you reach for enlightenment and even sanctity.

The second danger is of a different kind. Beware of religions as forms of holism, and especially of the fundamentalist variety. They offer you ready solutions for everything. But ultimately make you a prisoner of narrow dogmatic schemes.

The first danger consists of the fact that there is not enough scope and freedom for your spiritual development to go beyond and beyond in your journey of self-realization. The second danger is that your freedom may be taken away from you and ready solutions will be given to you; the "salvation" will be imposed on you. You then do not grow spiritually. You wither in the shadows of the dogmas. You need to discover your own of holistic understanding. And then proudly sail onto the sea of self-enlightenment.

Hope. is part of our ontological structure. Hope is a mode of our very being. To be alive is to live in a state of hope. Hope is a pre-condition of our mental health. Hope is the scaffolding of our existence.

Hope is the eternal flower that blossoms against the snow. Hope is the nourishment that sustains us daily. Hope is the oxygen for our hearts and souls. Hope is the ray of light that separates life from death.

Hope is a re-assertion of our belief in the meaning of human life; and in the sense of the universe. Hope is a pre-condition of all meaning, of all strivings, of all actions. To embrace hope is a form of wisdom; to abandon it is a form of foolishness.

The logic of hope is the logic of affirmation. The logic of hope is the logic of solidarity. The logic of hope is the logic of compassion. The logic of hope is the logic of courage. The logic of hope is the logic of responsibility. All these attributes: affirmation, solidarity, compassion, courage, responsibility are the very stuff of which life is made; that is life which is alive, life which leads to peace, harmony and wholeness.

Hope is courage, and courage does not have to be blind. Hope is affirmation, and affirmation does not have to be stupid. Hope is responsibility, and responsibility excludes ventures that are crazy or utterly impossible.

You cannot live by objectivity alone. But you can live by hope alone. Hope is not a spurious trapping, not a luxury but the very fountain of our inner life. What is left to human beings is hope. And love. Hope to sustain love. Love to sustain hope.

The logic of hope gives us the permission to be and become in the image of our transcendental self, in the image of our spiritual self, in the image of the person we ought to be. This is in consonance with Paul Tillich who maintained that the essence of the human being is not what he or she is but what a person can potentially become.

Wisdom precludes doom, gloom, pessimism, and apocaliptic visions of your own life and life at large. Wisdom is empowering. Wisdom is positive by its very nature. Wisdom is a vehicle of life ascending. Hope is its energizing source.

Courage. is this indomitable human quality without which life is a listless affair. Why should you have courage? Because you are human. What should you use your courage for? For living your life as an authentic being. True courage is not fighting in battles or performing acrobatic stunts. True courage is defending your integrity, your dignity, you inner sanctum. A supreme example of this courage is Socrates. With courage he fought for what was most important to him–his integrity and his inner sactum. He said during his trial to the judges of Athens. "Meletus and Anytus can kill me, but they cannot harm me." "This was a fantastic courage of living one's principles to the very end. This is the essential wisdom. For this reason Socrates behaviour stands as an epitomy of courage and wisdom.

Socrates could have escaped after he was sentenced; indeed was encouraged to do so. He chose to die—in order to enshrine the beauty of his life. And what would we have been without him doing so? What would we have been without the indomitable courage of Mother Teresa? What would we have been without the ceaseless courage of Mahatma Gandhi?

Take away courage and what is left of the human condition?

Take away courage and what is left of history? Take away courage and what is left of the individual life? An empty shell howling in its meaninglessness. To live in those outrageous and impossible times of ours requires courage, which is a pre-condition of the belief in the meaning of life.

Our faith in the meaning of life often crumbles. What saves us is an act of courage, which infuses us with the power and determination to go on. When this act falters, the meaning of our life totters. Courage is the fuel which renews the energy of our hope. Courage and hope are twin sisters.

Courage is part of the flame of wisdom. For wisdom has its flame. Fueled by courage our wisdom burns bright. Deprived of it, it totters. Wisdom almost wants to say: "give me courage or give me death."

Specific Strategies

We have reflected upon the hidden dimensions of human life which are invisible sources of sustenance, the deep pools of spiritual energy. By activating them, we enlarge our being. To embrace these hidden sources of sustenance and to cultivate them is wisdom itself. To forget or ignore them is unwisdom and darkness.

In addition to these lofty sources however we must find appropriate practices and meditations to cope with daily living, and in order to avoid–as much as possible–the many pitfalls and obstacles, which life is always putting on our path.

This section is more practical in character, as it tries to concentrate on strategies which enable us to overcome the various hurdles and traps on the way to wisdom. Let us be mindful that removing the obstacles is only clearing the way, not acquiring wisdom itself. We are smoothing the path so that the gentle and precious vehicle of wisdom rides on and does not get stuck.

The number of hurdles is countless. We shall not try to enumerate them all. Only several important ones will be discussed. Here they are.

(i) Don't be stupid.
(ii) Don't repeat the same mistakes.
(iii) The irritating situations.

(iv) Don't be preoccupied with trivia.
(v) Beyond the inner phobias, fears, anxiety.
(vi) Catharsis and forgiveness.
(vii) Discipline.

Don't be stupid. Don't repeat being stupid. This is the first step to becoming wise. We know when we act stupid. We are surprised with ourselves. And then act stupid again. You have to clearly catch yourself in acting unwise and say to yourself: Now I don't want this behaviour to be repeated. Then you must watch yourself. You must watch that which makes you act stupid.

It is a bad strategy in life to tolerate stupidity in our thought and behaviour, as if it were natural. Stupidity is natural at a very low level of consciousness. But not when you are on the path.

Repeating the same mistakes. Many times we do not act stupidly but somehow make the same mistakes. Watching over our life, we see a pattern of the same mistakes occurring, almost without our participation. Analyze the state of your being which allows these mistakes to happen. Prepare in advance for the situations in which they happen. Be watchful. Try to catch these mistakes before they have a chance to happen. When you are well familiar with the pattern, go deeper into yourself and find out what is it in your nature that *invites* these mistakes. There is probably some shadow within you which is causing the trouble. Gently bring this "shadow" to the full light. And then let it wither in the translucent light of your higher self.

These irritating situations. There are situations and people which constantly irritate you because of what they are. You wish that they just stop irritating you. They irritate you because of what they are. Is that right? Of course, you would say. Then think again. Nobody irritates you. You are irritating yourself–because of who you are. You need to defuse these fuses within you which make you irritated. You know how to do it if you go deeper into yourself. The same applies to anger, short temper, being mad with some people. These are all your little demons, your own creations, the result of impatience, lack of tolerance, lack of compassion.

Don't be preoccupied with trivia. Switch off this Television with its continuous chatter. Stop these silly conversations with others which are but words thrown to the wind.

Don't be preoccupied with your little dramas, which so often are but soap operas, and which take place in your mind over and again—adding nothing to you, but only draining your energy and clouding your larger perspectives and vistas. Why these little dramas repeat themselves is an interesting problem. But far more important is how to stop their continuous replay, so that your mind is freer for deeper things.

Stop these inner dialogues with yourself over things which have nothing to do with wisdom. These little obsessions may be interesting, perhaps even entertaining. But they are detrimental to wisdom in the long run.

Clearing your inner space of the trivial furniture is important. Wisdom requires spaciousness, distance, freedom from little annoyances which disturb the equilibrium of the mind and the equanimity of the soul.

Healing inner phobias, fears, anxieties. Let us go a step deeper and recognize that these frantic and fractured times of ours, full of uncertainty and violence, make us vuluerable. Life is vulnerable and frail. But it is also enduring and extremely adaptable.

Wisdom emphasizes the latter qualities, while so much of the pressure of the market place is targeted at your soft spots: of fear, anxiety and insecurity. While your soft spots are attacked, you feel even more vulnerable and insecure. If you don't do anything about it, the forces of the market place, including Television and media will play on your insecurities and anxieties forever.

Thus you must do something about it. You cannot allow yourself to be caught in the web of fears, anxieties and pananoias-which have nothing to do with your inner person. The inner person must prevail so that wisdom finds a suitable dwelling place in you.

Furthermore, by developing wisdom sufficiently, you will be able to subdue your anxieties and phobias, which are but little poodles which can bark (to disturb you) but cannot really bite.

So you need to stop these pangs of anxiety and these recurring waves of fear. There is nothing to fear about. Remember Socrates. He had no fears. Go to the source of your fears. You will find that they are fictions of your imagination. Release yourself from these imaginary ghosts.

But do it gently. First by serenely watching them and understanding their nature. Then smilingly saying to yourself: "Do I really need these little disturbing creatures?" Reflect. Then say firmly: "No, I don't need them": So you now tell them: "Go away. You may go away. You must go away." You are thereby sending them to some distant seas. Don't fight with them. Don't get angry with yourself, when they refuse to go. This will only entrench their position inside you. Gently say to yourself: "O.K. if you don't want to go all at once, I shall disinvite you one by one, by giving you less and less time, until you are gone. But you must be quite firm and systematic in disinviting them. And occasionally you need to flush them out of your system by appropriate visualization meditations. May they dissolve in some distant seas.

Catharsis and forgiveness. You are articulating your larger self as a part of your pursuit of wisdom. This requires clearing a lot of rubble from your inner house. Catharsis, which is a beautiful Greek term denoting cleansing and purification, is a necessary process for the pursuit of wisdom. The state of wisdom signifies integrity, radiance, beauty, harmony. But also a certain purity of the beholder of wisdom. You cannot arrive at the gates of the temple of wisdom stained and sullied, with dust and pollution all over you and inside you.

Hence you undergo catharsis. Catharsis is ultimately cleaning your soul, heart and mind. The various strategies we have proposed are but steps of this larger process of catharsis.

This process of cleansing also includes forgiveness, especially those who (you think) hurt you most. The memory of these hurts may still be sore spots on your heart and soul. You must heal the scars and the sore spots. You must forgive so that these unnecessary memories are released and go to some distant seas. You must forgive for your own sake. Through forgiveness, the painful spots will be cured. Forgiving is a part of catharsis, cleaning your system of unnecessary psychic balast.

Also remember: Don't try to make other people understand you. You are here to understand them. May you be mindful that those who understand more understand these who understand less. But those who understand less do not understand these who under stand more. Understanding is a profound process. It requires wisdom, compassion and sometimes a deep insight. Try to understand that compassion is a form of understanding. Compassion is also a form of healing. True catharsis always involves compassion.

Discipline. In whatever you do, don't forget about the right discipline. When a wrestler or an athlete builds his body, he endures a systematic training over months and years. It is a conscious and continuous effort.

Spiritual work requires discipline—a continuous and conscious effort—over a long period of time. Don't fool yourself that you can make much spiritual advancement in your "spare time." You must set for yourself special exercises, like the athletes do, and then watch yourself in order to see whether you are moving forward. We are talking about a gentle discipline not some kind of Prussian drill. Discipline means first of all preventing yourself from self-indulgence, to which we are prone.

So watch yourself. But don't watch how much wiser you are becoming daily or monthly. Watch rather how much less stupid, indolent and self-centered you are becoming.

Also watch how much more serene and inwardly connected you are. Never forget about the right discipline. Make it a part of the habit of your life. Then you are on the path of wisdom.

The Gifts of Wisdom

Wisdom enlarges your being. But it also diminishes your smallness, your confinment, your self-centeredness. You cannot truly enlarge your being while you are still stuck in your little puddles of selfishness, envy, grasping for personal advantage. Thus the arrival of wisdom simultanously signifies the shrinking of your small self. The two processes run parallel to each other. The more wisdom you behold, the less silliness there is in you. And the reverse is also true. The more silliness there is in you, the less wisdom you can behold.

As you acquire wisdom and enlarge your being, many old selfish trappings wither away. And they have to. Because it is the nature of wisdom to dissolve your narrowness, ego-centricity, the peculiar blindness which focuses entirely on yourself.

So, the first benefit of wisdom is that it brings you liberation from your own individual confinment.

The second important gift of wisdom is that it offers itself as an aid to life. It is not a strait jacket which cramps your life and makes it a burden. Wisdom is wings. Wisdom is joy. Wisdom is a passage to these higher realms of self-fulfilment, which cannot be achieved by following the ordinary path of a merely material existence. Wisdom makes you sublime. In this state of sublimity, you become impervious (at least to a large degree) to the slings and arrows of the blind shooters of their own misfortunes.

Wisdom helps us to navigate ourselves in this vast sea of social, ecological and cultural relationships by which we are surrounded. Wisdom transcends ordinary knoweldge, especially bookish knowledge, but is itself a form of knowledge, albeit guided by our inner light and larger visions of the destiny of humanity.

Wisdom is the possession of the right knowledge, but for a given state of the world, for given conditions of society, for given articulation of the human condition. In so far as the state of the world changes, in so far as the conditions of society change, in so far as human mind and human sensitivities become refined, we cannot embrace one structure of wisdom for all times. We must seek a different structure, a different form of balance for each epoch. You cannot be a student of wisdom and acquire wisdom. Acquiring wisdom is like sculpting the inner man.

Wisdom is therefore a historical category, not a set of permanent forms but a set of dynamic structures; always to be re-built, re-structured, re-adjusted, re-articulated. Evolutionary wisdom is understanding how the human condition changes through centuries, millennia, aeons of time. Only such a conception of wisdom can aid the race in its evolutionary journey.

Thus first of all we must strive to understand the living wisdom; not dead wisdom of old musty books not petrified wisdom of antiquated precepts, but this living flame which sustains and guides us in daily living. The living flame is carried on from generation to generation, sustained by human dreams and visions, and this peculiar energy which we call spiritual energy.

Living wisdom is evolutionary wisdom. As we evolve, the conditions of the world and of our being evolve and change. And so this knowledge which we call the living flame of wisdom also changes.

It is indeed wise to recognise the nature of evolutionary wisdom. It is indeed wise not to cling to old antiquated principles but to cultivate the living flame of which we are a part.

The third magnificent gift of wisdom is that it offers itself as stepping stones to enlightenment and divinity. Wisdom represents a ladder to heaven—at least the first part of it. When we submerge ourselves deep enough in the folds of wisdom, we touch the inaffable, we merge with the inaffable. Wisdom is divine because it helps us to understand divinity, and is itself a vehicle of a divine nature.

At one point of our journey of pursuing wisdom, we recognize, with joy and elation, that our quest is to reach the transcendent beauty of the universe and of our own being. We recognize the latent divinity in ourselves and in the whole creation. We desire to embrace divinity because we are of it. We desire to become it because such is the deepest quest of our soul. Our wisdom has become the light of revelation of the inaffable.

This state of our being is essentially beyond wisdom, yet it is of wisdom. It is deliverence of wisdom, deliverence of light through wisdom, deliverence of us to the gates of heaven.

We know that there are stages beyond wisdom. Self-realization is the next. Enlightenment is further still. And divinity transcends enlightenment. But wisdom is a necessary path to all of them.

Without attempting to be dogmatic about these matters—for we find ourselves in a subtle realm, where words are woefully inadequate—we might wish to say that self-realization is the fruit of wisdom. When you are self-realized, you have passed through the gates of wisdom. You cannot be self-realized without being wise.

Perhaps it is similar on the still higher reaches of our journey. If you are enlightened you are self-realized. But the reverse is not true. If you are self-realized, you are not necessarily enlightened. As we said, we are in a subtle and profound territory here. We don't wish to rely too much on words. We are beyond words. The alpha bet, grammar and syntax of our higher states of being can only be conveyed in silence, deep mediatation, the whispers of our soul, and these harmonies of the cosmos which we call divine.

The process of the acquisition of wisdom takes time. For it is a process of sculpting the inner person. Sculpting in marble is difficult enough. But sculpting the human soul is far more difficult. For the substance we handle is so delicate, fragile and elusive. It refuses to be forced in any prefabricated moulds. Yet it needs to acquire distinctive shapes.

Thus the process of sculpting takes time. Therefore, allow yourself two to twenty years to acquire wisdom, to shape yourself into a sculpture of wisdom. If you think that you don't have this time, and that you must rush, then you don't want to acquire wisdom and be truly a wise person.

You may be already advanced on the path of wisdom, and you only need some refining touches. That is another matter. Or you may be about ready to enter the next stage of self-realization. If so, good journey—to these more rarified regions and peaks.

Wisdom is important. But it is not the end of the journey. Only a stage in this most enthralling of the human endeavours called reaching the abode of gods.

Chapter 6

Universal Compassion and the Ecological Dharma

Ecology as a Religious Responsibility

On September 26, 1986, thousands of people from all over the world came to Assisi and filled the Basilica of St. Francis and the surrounding area. This was not the periodic annual pilgrimage on St. Francis' birthday. The occasion was much more auspicious. Five major religions-Buddhism, Christianity, Hinduism, Judaism and Islam-came together in a spirit of unprecedented harmony, to pledge their allegiance to the Earth. During the Assisi Congress it was declared, and since reiterated, that the well-being of the Earth, and its preservation for the sake of future generations, is a spiritual responsibility for all religions.

Religious people disagree on many points. But on this issue they all seem to be in emphatic agreement: that the healing and the preservation of the Earth is our common responsibility, not only for our economic benefit (so that the Earth continues to feed us), but out of our understanding of the holiness of the planet and all its creatures.

To worship God truly in our times is to save the planet. If we lose the environment, we lose God. Healing both the planet and ourselves has today become spiritual work of the first magnitude. Whatever our race and religion, ecology connects us all together. Thus ecology is the religious project of our times. The idea of redemption acquires a new meaning: it means redeeming the world by healing the Earth, since healing the Earth is the spiritual work of our time. This means that to understand religious devotion is to recognize that all religions are forms of worshipping the beauty and integrity of the planet.

This approach could be a point of departure and renewal for many spiritual traditions. It could be the basis for our unity. And what could be more worthy of our collective purpose than working together to save our Earth and implicitly ourselves?

Without the vibrant Earth we shall cease to exist.

Spirituality is also, and has always been, the realization of our inner potential, the actualization of the God within us. We need to treat each other according to what we can potentially become: divine lights uplifting ourselves and helping others to heal. to integrate, to become more reverential. But working on ourselves to release and articulate our inner divinity, and working in the outside world to heal the Earth are *complementary* aspects of ecological spirituality. Instead of the quietistic forms of spirituality which are favoured by many religions, this involves a participatory form of spirituality, a spirituality which resolves itself in the acts of healing in everyday life.

Part of this new spirituality, which I call ecological spirituality, is a new kind of prayer, which I call ecological prayer. Praying to Absolute Deities endowed with divine attributes is well and good. But to save the integrity and beauty of creation, we need to be engaged in ecological prayer. Ecological prayer is acting out the ecological dimension of our existence, and bringing all beings into the campus of our well-wishing. It is bringing a meditative attitude to our daily activities which helps to heal on all levels of being, and is thus a form of ethics in action, based on solidarity and on compassion, and leading to a larger harmony in the long run.

It should be clear that ecological spirituality has a distinctively practical dimension, continually asking us the following question: How do you work on yourself so that you heal within? So that you heal your mind? So that you become a source of health and support for others? How do you help to heal the diseased educational system, the malfunctioning and carcinogenic social and political structures? How do you help to heal the Earth in your immediate vicinity? How can your lifestyle help to maintain the equilibrium in distant parts of the world by not contributing to frivolous over-consumption?

All these questions are both practical and spiritual at the same time. They require a new kind of awareness, a new kind of commitment, a new kind of yoga. What I am describing is a common religious project for our times. Let us unite together in the common service to Mother Earth, in one stupendous ecological prayer. Then the gods will help us. We need to help the gods so that they can help us. We need to engage in Ecological Dharma, so that the Buddhas bless us in this new holy act. We need to help God-of the Hebrews, Christians, and Muslims-so that God helps us to make God's Earth green and blessed again.

A New Response is Required to the Principle of Non-Attachment

As we examine the causes of the ecological crisis, we realize that we are truly in an unprecedented and precarious situation. Not only have we upset the natural balance of the Earth so that renewal has become difficult. We have also caused immense suffering to the Earth, to all its creatures, and to human beings. This is a new form of suffering, of a kind and on a scale unknown in earlier times.

We have invented so many chemicals which are added to the products we use daily: the food we eat, the fabrics we wear, the paints we use in our houses. So many of these chemicals have a poisonous residue. We are being slowly poisoned in a subtle but unprecedented way. Our health is being undermined, our well-being diminished, our worries and anxieties increased. The diseases of civilization are afflicting more and more people even (and especially!) in prosperous countries.

The lifestyle which accompanies the ecological crisis is one of continuous tension, which comes about as a result of the omnipresence of stress. Stress is one of the new forms of suffering and a killer in our times. Systematic poisoning of various kinds (of food, of the air, of the water we drink) and systematic stress which seems to be people's daily companion, cause a deep sea of suffering unknown in previous history. We must be able to address ourselves to this suffering in a relevant way.

Let me share a story with you from Poland, the country to which I recently returned to settle, after having spent thirty years in the West, mainly in the USA. In the 1970's Poland embarked on an enormous venture of industrialization: giant steel mills and petrochemical factories. This was meant to be progress, catching up with the prosperous West. But the consequences have been disastrous. Poland is now one of the most polluted countries in Europe, with some regions nothing short of an ecological catastrophe. In the South-West part of the country there is a triangle of three cities (Chorzow, Katowice, Bytom) which is called the triangle of death. 25 percent of children up to the age of eighteen need special medical attention. They were born impaired. Many children are born dead. Many are born so deformed that they appear like little monsters. Many of the children are mentally crippled. Some are aware of their plight. They even plead with normal people: "Please do not treat us like idiots. We just have too much lead in our brains." We may recall that the Roman aristocracy drank their wine out of lead cups, while ordinary people drank it out of ceramic cups. We cannot be sure how much this lead poisoning diminished their intelligence, or led to the fall of the Roman Empire.

As compassionate beings who wish, and have the duty, to help other sentient beings, we cannot be oblivious towards those new forms of suffering. Ecological prayer is a new form of prayer, and it outlines a new form of dharma, the dharma of healing and caring for the Earth.

During a dialogue with Tibetan Buddhists at Dharamsala in April 1991, I chose as my main subject Ecological Dharma. I proposed that dharma in our times acquires a distinctly green shade, an ecological dimension. It is not sufficient nowadays to take care of our spiritual well-being, to care about our religious community. We must extend this care to the entire Earth. For this is our dwelling, our temple, our sangha, our vessel in which spiritual attainments can be perfected on the way to becoming a *bodhisattva*. I suggested at this meeting that we cannot afford to be too detached nowadays. The principle of non-attachment is, of course, beautiful and important. Yet we need to re-examine its meaning, precisely because of the importance of Ecological Dharma. **We cannot be too detached from the Earth, because then we can lose the Earth all together**. We need to cling to the Earth. Now the idea of clinging to the Earth and of questioning the principle of non-attachment alarmed many of the learned monks present at the symposium. The opposition to this idea became so heated that I was bound to say: "You seem to be very attached to your principle of non-attachment." The monks got my point immediately.

Needless to say, we have to tread very carefully when we

propose "clinging to the Earth" and when we propose a re-examination of the principle of non-attachment. Yet the main point I wish to make is this: We need to cling to the Earth much more passionately than we cling to traditional scriptures. This point applies to all religions. Clinging to the scriptures while the Earth is in distress may not be the appropriate way of participating in divinity.

How should we view the principle of non-attachment in our times? It can be viewed either as a renunciation of the world, or as deeper participation in the world. The Buddha himself chose the latter course. He decided to stay, to help others in relieving their suffering and in aiding their quest for enlightenment. Other great lights such as Zoroaster, Mahavira or Jesus chose a similar course. There have been some great lights who so completely renounced the world that we never heard from them again. We salute their single-mindedness. But we also observe that, by choosing an austere course, which could be interpreted as a special form of non-attachment, they apparently did not help other human beings.

To whom do we owe the greatest allegiance — to our own divinity, or to the divinity of the world as expressed through other beings? This is an eternal question which split Buddhism into the Hinayana and the Mahayana schools. Ideally we would wish to say that we owe our allegiance to both, particularly as our own divinity is a part of the divinity of the world. Yet in practical life, we have to make choices, and so the path of inner liberation is often pursued at the expense of helping the world, or vice-versa.

When our house in completely in order, we have no fear of attachment, and we are not threatened when the principle of non-attachment is questioned. The dharma of the *bodhisattva* redeems the world or at least relieves the suffering of others. This Dharma is not afraid of being in the world, with the world, as it absorbs the suffering of the world: the *bodhisattva* walks on water while not being drawn into it.

The Dharma of wholeness

In recent years, our understanding of the world has changed. In many ways, this understanding has been impoverished, and in many ways, it has been deepened. As astrophysics and the new physics reveal to us the depth of the universe, as we grapple with the idea of the beginning of time, as we begin to appreciate the wonderful alchemy of the universe in the making, we cannot but gasp in wonder. The stories of contemporary science reveal to us new dimensions of the sacredness of the universe. We see that the whole process of the unfolding of the universe has been so exquisite, the forces that have balanced it so delicate, the transfiguration of matter into spirit so relentless and yet so subtle, that we have every reason to feel that we are in one enormous sacred temple. Astrophysicists tell us that the universe is home for human beings. We can go a step further and maintain that the universe is a sanctuary and that we are its keepers, custodians, trustees.

Thus participating in this universe is participating in its divinity. When the world is considered a sordid place, then withdrawal from it, or non-attachment, is commendable. But when the whole world is viewed as divine, participation in it is holy and commendable. This is the new dharma of wholeness : the participation in the whole divinity of the universe. The Bodhisattva in our times is a custodian in the sanctuary which is the universe.

The Unavoidability of Suffering

Whenever possible, suffering should be diminished. Spurious, crushing suffering should be eliminated. Yet not all suffering can be eliminated, nor should it be. Yes, we aim at the reduction of suffering, and we even talk about the total elimination of suffering as if this were desirable. But it is not. Can we imagine the world totally void of suffering? What kind of place would that be? A kind of plastic, one-dimensional universe. Can we imagine human beings growing into maturity and depth without any suffering? What kind of beings would those be, ones who never suffered?

Suffering is the source of deeper understanding and compassion, the spring out of which grows wisdom and ultimately enlightenment. So suffer we must. Can we imagine the Buddha himself announcing the Four Noble Truths and the Eightfold Path without previous suffering? What was necessary for the Buddha in order to acquire wisdom, compassion and enlightenment, is necessary for us too. No one can suffer for us to make us wise and enlightened. The enlightened ones, the *avatars*, show the way. But they cannot be our saviors, for in releasing us from our responsibility, they would bar our path to true wisdom and enlightenment.

Would there be enlightenment if there were no obstacles? The idea of suffering, as a prerequisite of wisdom and enlightenment, leads us to the simple realization that wisdom and enlightenment are human attributes. And so the human species strives for these amidst obstacles and suffering.

The New Eightfold Path

In order to understand the nature of suffering in our times, we need to understand how we have increased and multiplied suffering through the onslaught of technology, through poisoning the water, the air, our food, our minds. This suffering is reverberating throughout the whole planet and the lives of its creatures. In those parts of the world where we created affluence through technology and material progress, we also brought about new forms of suffering-the diseases of civilization. The shorthand term for these new forms of suffering is the ecological blight.

It thus follows that ecological cleansing will lead to the cessation of suffering. Ecology is the noble truth of our times, as we attempt to eliminate an enormous sea of suffering caused by people's unwisdom and concomitant greed, quest for power, and loss of hope.

We ourselves are often the murderer's apprentices, as we contribute through our work, research or teaching to the ecological destruction of the planet. So we need to reflect very carefully on the Eightfold Path in order to give it a distinctly green shade, at least as far as the first five principles are concerned.

Our belief systems, and thus our thought structures, have been profoundly influenced by Western rationality, and Western conceptions of the world as a machine to be controlled and manipulated through our knowledge. This belief system has become our second nature. It is reflected in our language and in our action.

This whole thought structure (or the mechanistic world-view) has been destructive to the environment and to our psyche. This we know. By living inside the machine we have created, our beliefs (assumptions), our thought, our speech, our conduct (action) and ultimately our livelihood have all been affected. The way to escape the machine is not to go backwards, to pre-scientific cultures. We have to leap forward, transcend it. I have tried to do so through an eco-philosophy which spells out a distinctive ecological cosmology (right beliefs, right thought, right speech) and a distinctive ecological ethics (right conduct, right livelihood). According to eco-cosmology, the world is not a machine but a *sanctuary*. This immediately redefines a multitude of things. The human person is no longer seen as a machinist, who manipulates or is manipulated, but as a custodian and guardian of the planet, and everything in the universe. From this conception of the cosmos (and of the human being within it) follows an ethics of reverence, responsibility, frugality, and justice. We need a positive ecological path, which will merge with the traditional Eightfold Path and transform it in the process.

Technological progress has forced us out of our natural niches. We are lost in concrete jungles. We find it more and more difficult to pursue right livelihood. Thus, one of the great problems of our time is to reverse the trend which forces people to do meaningless jobs which by and large are destructive to the environment. Right livelihood is not just an economic problem. Wrong livelihood is destroying people's souls and is undermining the sustainability of the planet. The Buddha was absolutely correct in seeing right livelihood as spiritual proposition essential to our rightful destiny.

The Ecological Dharma informs us that ecological reconstruction, working close to nature, bringing back labour-intensive occupations, and working in general for ecological catharsis, is the road which leads us to the fold of right livelihood. Thus, the Ecological Dharma appears to be an essential vehicle for bringing us back to right livelihood which is so essential to our spiritual well-being. Unless we find the road reconnecting us with right livelihood-not only for a select few but for countless millions-we cannot claim that our spiritual message is relevant to the present time.

All religions and spiritual traditions are somewhat at a loss in the face of our ecological plight. Buddhism is no exception, although admittedly it does seem better prepared for handling the difficult tasks than most other traditions. There are clear reasons for this. It was based on a deeper and more encompassing vision that Christianity (Buddhism has been inclusive rather than exclusive, while both Judaism and Christianity have traditionally been exclusive); it was cosmos-centred by comparison with Christianity which was centred on the relation of individual vis-a-vis God; and it conceived of responsibility in global and universal terms, in terms of universal karma, while both Judaism and Christianity have tended to be more parochial, relating karma too closely to our individual sins.

In summary, our times call for new resources of imagination and inner power to respond to the unprecedented peril to the life of the planet and to our own spiritual lives. These two are aspects of one another. Clearly, a new Ecological Dharma is called for. This dharma requires of us to be passionately attached to the Earth, which of course does not mean the childish clinging to material possessions or to consumption. The practice of universal compassion in our times requires a work of ecological reconstruction and ecological healing unprecedented in history. As the ecological crisis has brought about an enormous sea of new suffering, ecological cleansing becomes the vehicle of the cessation of this suffering. Ecology is the nobel truth of our times.

In responding to the present crisis we need to be strengthened by the flame of enduring spiritual traditions, for we remember that thousands of candles can be lighted from a single candle, without the life of the candle being shortened. Yet, we also remember that even the Buddhas can only point the way. The rest of the journey we have to travel ourselves, in a new terrain unknown to previous epochs with pitfalls and traps that often boggle the imagination. We need to have strength and vision, for our journey may be decisive to future generations.

Notes

1. See Henryk Skolimowski, *Living Philosophy: Eco-philosophy as a Tree of Life*, (London Penguin Books, Arkana Series, 1992) which gives positive guidelines for action and livelihood.
2. For further discussion see my *Dancing Shiva in the Ecological Age* (New Delhi: Clarion Books, 1991).

Chapter 7

On The Significance Of Ecophilosophy

Ecology Has Come of Age

Ecology is in vogue nowadays. It was not so when I started ploughing the virgin fields of eco-philosophy; and even after I published the first book in the field, in 1981, under the title *Eco-philosophy, Designing is New Tactics for Living*. The subtitle is significant. It was significant then, and it is significant now. We are designing new tactics clear living, not just spinning out new philosophical abstractions. The term "Eco-friendly" is now commonly used, and even abused. It does not bother me that is abused. There must be an underlying substratum of meaning and of energy which makes people resonate with the term "Eco-friendly". Thus, it is a nice term, but it does not go very far.

I was at Gandhi Niketan Ashram deep in Southern India, near Madurai, some time ago. The Secretary of the Ashram was curious about Eco-Philosophy. But a bit sceptical too. He asked me directly: "What is the difference between 'Eco-friendly' and 'Eco-philosophy'? There was a genuine curiosity expressed in the question, but also a bit of scepticism. I responded to him equally succinctly and said: "Eco-philosophy is Eco-friendly and it knows why". This '*why*' is every important. To answer this why adequately is to reveal the whole drama of the present technological civilisation. And also to reveal a lumious promise of recovery from present debacles. We must know what we are doing and why. And this 'why' must go rather deep. Otherwise our Eco-friendly talk will be but a friendly chat.

The question 'why' has many levels of depth and many ramifications. I will address some of these levels by asking the two basic questions. I will first answer these questions succinctly, and then I will attempt to provide in-depth answers.

(i) Why has Eco-philosophy emerged?
Because the mechanistic experiment has failed.

(ii) Why is Eco-philosophy important?

Beause we are starved of meaning and of spiritual nourishment; because it attempts to restore the balance between the human and the rest of creation.

Let me now respond to each of these questions at some length, starting with the first. I have said that Eco-philosophy is emerging as we clearly witness the twilight of the mechanistic experiment.

The Myth of the Machine

It was a great act of imagination to conceive of the universe as a huge machine moving according tot he predetermined mechanistic laws. It was a great act of courage to follow through this mechanistic design for three centuries to its bitter end. And thirdly, it was a great act of folly to assume that there is nothing of importance in the universe except matter and its mechanistic laws; and that the phenomenon of man can be explained through these mechanistic laws. Human diligence and human folly are two sides of the same coin.

Now after three centuries of pursuing this most splendid of Western invention - the invention of the world as a clock like mechanism - we stand in front of its ruins, gasping in disbelief. After the story has run its course, we are shocked! Instead of the Splendid New World, in which everybody is fulfilled and happy, we have created the paranoic world of insecurity and increasing violence, while causing immense suffering to the earth itself and its creatures.

Let us examine the story in a systematic way and try to answer in which way or in what sense the mechanic experiment has failed.

It has failed *firstly* in its very conception of the universe. It has claimed that the universe is a huge clock-like mechanism, whose behaviour can be satisfactory, if not completely, explained by the mechanistic and deterministic laws. For two centuries it appeared that the mechanistic design was the most adequate way of reading the nature of nature. Sir Issac Newton considered himself a favourite prophet of God. He was offended when people questioned the veracity of his mechanistic laws. He considered these laws to be given by God. And the purpose of these laws was to uniquely express the architecture of the universe. These were meant to be God's Laws explaining the physical behaviour of nature. Furthermore, it was with God's blessing that Newton was allowed to unevil the new Grand Design.

Such was the state of things throughout the 18th Century and almost through the 19th Century. Newton's laws were considered the laws of nature. The greatest minds, including the minds of such powerful and incisive philosophers as Boruch Spinoza (1632-77) and Immanuel Kant (1720-1804) did not dare to question or challenge the sacred dogmas of Newton. Of course, the philosophers of the FrenchEnlightenment, such as D'Alambert, Diderot, Voltaire (but not Rousseau!) accepted the dogmas with relish and built on it their specific dogmas: of Progress, of Reason, of Liberty.

Then towards the end of the 19th Century things started to happen. Radio-activity was discovered, which did not fit at all into the mechanistic scheme. Electro-magnetism was discovered, which was an awkward fellow in the Newtonian universe. Then in the 20th Century the solid walls of the Newtonian universe started to crumble in many places. First came Einstein's blow - the theory of relativity. Then another blow - Quantum Theory, which has given rise to Quantum Physics. Then an avalanche of new theories followed to which the common name of the New Physics was given.

The net result is that the mechanistic design is in ruins. In the cosmological sense the mechanistic experiment has clearly and utterly failed. There is no doubting it whatsoever.

We no longer talk about the *laws of nature*. We no longer talk about scientific theories. We talk only about scientific hypotheses. We talk about conjectures, something tentative and frail, established for the time being, and not for all times. We have become humble. We no longer claim that we know reality. Scientists nowadays are shy in talking about reality and in claiming that science describes reality adequately and objectively. We increasingly talk about the participatory universe. We talk about the participatory mind. In this participatory universe we co-create with reality via the participatory mind. Reality is thus participatory, not objective. In the realm of sub-atomic physics, we have created a fluid universe of Dancing Shiva which is vastly different from the Newtonian Universe of hard billiard balls moving inexorably according to the mechanistic and deterministic laws. This is then the first reason for the collapse of the mechanistic experiment - it has crumbled under its own accumulated strains. The cosmological structure it has provided proved to be inadequate and illusory in its permanency.

Let me now explain the *second reason* for the failure of the mechanistic experiment. This experiment has failed because the idea of *Progress*, conceived as the vehicle which delivers fulfilment and happiness to all has failed. This is the second ground for the collapse of the mechanistic scheme. Let us be clearly aware that the mechanistic design was not only a cosmological matrix. It was also an *eschatological* scheme. It attempted to provide the salvation, here on earth, through material satisfaction.

The mechanistic laws of the universe meant to explain the behaviour of physical bodies. But more than that. They alsc explained how to *manipulate* the universe, and then how to control it to our advantage. Manipulation and control of the physical universe became woven into the over-all structure of the mechanistic scheme. This manipulation and control were meant to subdue nature to serve our ends. In Francis Bacon's ill-fated words, we meant to rape nature to serve us. All these strategies were conceived to serve the God of material progress. For indeed progress has become a deity for Western people. Until recently progress was sacrosanct, particularly for the people educated in Western universities, controlled by scientific rationality and inspired by the idea that knowledge is power.

Then in the 1960's the myth of progress started to wane rapidly. And so much so that in some quarters it had become a dirty word. Why so? For several reasons. Progress has not delivered. It has not lived up to its promise. And the promise was to make people all over the globe fulfilled and happy. This has not happened. And this is not going to happen. Thus progress is not the kind of vehicle we once deemed it to be-the vehicle leading to universal prosperity, peace and happiness. Even in the countries in which progress has celebrated its undoubted successes, in which material prosperity has risen phenomenally, the total balance sheet is abysmal : existential and spiritual misery, strife and stress ridden societies, violence on the streets and within families.

Secondly, progress has been discredited because we now see clearly that it has been used as an ideological weapon of the imperialist expansion of the West. To exploit less developed countries economically, Western people brought the Trojan Horse called the gospel of progress. In the name of this gospel, the industrial West has devastated the natural environment of under developed countries, their traditional sustainable agriculture, their well tried cultural and religious patterns. This sinister legacy of progress is now seen for what it is.

The third reason why progress is now viewed with dismay in the existential and spiritual plight of people, particularly in the West, who toiled and sweated, sacrificing their life and allowed themselves to be used in the name of progress. And then they found themselves empty handed, with a bitter taste in their mouths. Fulfilment and happiness did not arrive. Progress has turned out to be a false god.

In summary, the idea of progress is now viewed very critically because this great deity of the Western mind has not led us to the promised land. Instead it has led us to the barren land of ecological devastation. This in itself is a sufficient reason to seek, as the basis for our thinking, a new philosophy which is non-destructive and which promises man's reconciliation with nature.

I now come to the *third reason* responsible for the collapse of the mechanistic scheme. The first reason was cosmological - the structure of the cosmos proposed by mechanistic philosophy turned out to be lamentably inadequate. The second reason was eschatological - the form of salvation progress has promised turned into poisonous chalice. The third reason is as follows. The idea of man as independent of God(s), man as ruler over all there is - has misfired.

The mechanistic scheme has been a vast enterprise. It

spelt out not only the structure of the cosmos; not only the idea of progress, but also a specific concept of man. In the universe in which progress is conceived as the force that delivers us to the gates of paradise, we don't need God, we don't need sancity, we don't need spiritual nourishment. Science and technology deliver all that is necessary and sufficient for the fulfillment of man. Paradise is here on earth and not in some transcendent heaven. Thus we don't need God, we don't need other temples, save the supermarkets; we don't need spirituality, conceived as the nourishment of the soul. Progressively the human being is denuded of deeper layers of his existence. Starved spiritually and existentially at the end of the cycle we witness an alienated, empty and frustrated being, confused, and not understanding what has happened.

Now the rationality of the Brave Mechanistic World has continually maintained that we live in a very rational world; and in fact in the best of all possible worlds. This, it turned out to be an illusion. Thus on the third count, the mechanistic experiment has failed because inadvertently it produced the one-dimentional man who is the master of his technological follies while he himself is shrivelled in his existential miseries.

The *fourth* reason for the failure of the mechanistic experiment is *ecological*. Driven by the imperatives of the mechanistic world-view, man's relationship with nature has been strained to the breaking point. We have not only devastated the environment. We have estranged ourselves from nature. This estrangement from nature is part of our estrangement from our spiritual nature. We need nature for breathing with our lungs. But we also need nature for the breathing of our souls. In the tranquillity of forests and the majesty of rugged mountains, our soul sings or alternatively rests in a deep primordial silence. And this silence is important to our well being. Disturbing our relationship with nature so deeply could not but result in a deep disturbance of our psyche. The mechanistic scheme does not understand how deep and subtle are our relationships with the infinite riches of the cosmos. Therefore when it is on its romp of conquest, it is oblivious of the deeper consequences that follow. It is not a truism to repeat that we are a part of nature and nature is a part of us. By cutting nature mercilessly, the mechanistic progress has been cutting us. Thus the mechanistic scheme has failed profoundly while alienating us from nature and therefore from ourselves. In brief, the whole mechanistic philosophy has failed and we must seek a new one.

The Dawn of a New Philosophy : The World as Sanctuary.

Criticism per se is barren. It does not lead by itself to new constructive solutions. Yet we needed to take a critical view of the mechanistic scheme because it has been so overwhelming and so incapacitating. The reasons are now clear and sufficient to declare the mechanistic philosophy to be bankrupt. Post modernism is not an answer. It is itself a strange decadent dance on the ruins of the modern world view.

We need a new philosophy. We need a new philosophy not only to understand the world better. We need a new philosophy because we cannot live in a meaningless universe; because we are starved of the spiritual nourishment; because we need to rebuild our humanity which is an empty skeleton without any spiritual substance.

Understanding the world around us is important. But our understanding will always be partial and inadequate. Consequently the understanding of the physical world is just one thing. For more important is the understanding of our spiritual nature and providing the fuel for our soul. Why is eco-philosophy important? (We are addressing our second major question). Because it answers our spiritual quest. Because it restores the balance between the human and the rest of creation. Because it finds for the human a new meaningful place in this universe so that the universe becomes home for man. Eco-philosophy does provide a new cosmology and consequently gives us a new perspective on the physical world; as well as unveils a new participatory model for the interaction of the human with the participatory universe. These aspects of Eco-philosophy I have discussed at length in my books: *Living Philosophy* (1992) and *The Participatory Mind* (1994). In this discourse I address myself mainly to the spiritual character of Eco-philosophy in order to show how it fills the meaning vacuum, how it is spiritually nourishing, how it connects us with heaven and our inner God.

Where do we begin? By postulating that the *world is sanctuary*. This is the central point of departure of Eco-philosophy, its foundation pillar. The assumption that the world is sanctuary does not need to be justified or proved. It is much more intuitive than the assumption that the world is a machine; and actually in congruence with the great cultural and spiritual traditions of human kind. Besides, basic cosmological presuppositions are never proven. They are assumed. Then we build on them. Their worth is finally shown by the consequences that follow from them later; sometimes centuries later. Greatest religious traditions have proven their worth because for millennia their presuppositions (roots of the spiritual nourishment) have shown to be sustainable to human beings.

From the idea that the world is sanctuary there immediately follows that we are the guardians of the sanctuary; some even would want to say the priests in the sanctuary. Our inevitable response to the world which is a sanctuary is: reverence and responsibility. This reverence embraces nature and all there is in the universe. All is sacred, endowed with divinity, part of the sanctuary.

In this new world, we do not need to desperately search for meaning. We are each of us a santuary, a sacred vessel. Being aware of our extraordinary status as shepherds of beings, as guardians of our own sanctuary, (and of the great sanctuary of the cosmos), is a source of a great joy, of fulfillment. For in maintaining the sanctuaries we are doing something immensely important. We are self-realising ourselves while taking care of sanctuaries.

The sanctuary of nature is one of them. We treat nature and natural systems reverentially because they are a part of the Great Sanctuary. We also take exquisite care of sanctum sanctorum, our inner sanctuary, the god-within. Taking care of this sanctuary gives us an immense joy because it is most unique of the sanctuaries.

In brief, we no longer need to search for meaning because maintaining sanctuaries fills us with deep meaning. We no longer seek spiritual nourishment because we are continually nourished by the great source of energy.

Among our sources are great souls of the past, mahatmas,

saints, rishis, who are reservoirs of spiritual energy, who are ready to give us energy, through their teaching, if we are open, receptive and sensitive to receive it. Maintaining sanctuaries is not a pious act of sweeping the invisible spiritual dust from traditional temples, but it signifies opening up to the glory of the cosmic forces and singing with the universe the great song of creation.

The spiritual song of the universe is not some faint noise on the periphery of the immense throttle of the machine. This song is of the essence to the meaning of the universe. Whoever has opened himself to the divine energies of the cosmos is lucidly aware how shabby and incomplete is the universe without the spiritual dimensions. The re-enchantment of the world, re-acquiring meaning in our life, nourishing our spiritual nature are all connected within the grand design of the spiritual tapestry. Maintaining sanctuaries is maintaining this tapestry. We are its weavers and the threads of which it is woven. The enduring beauty of this tapestry is what makes life worth living, what makes life endurable, what makes life singing.

Let me now summarise the basic features and the uniqueness of Eco-philosophy.

I. *It is a holistic philosophy.* Yet we must remember that it is holistic in a post mechanistic and post analytical era. Therefore it is not afraid of analysis and rationality. On the contrary, it uses them to show that holistic philosophy is rational; and that the holistic way of life is the only one that can be rationally justified.

II. *It is reverential towards nature and towards all creation.* This reverence is born not out of soapy sentimentality, but of luminous realisation that we are an inherent aspect of the web of life. To use the memorable words of the Chief Seattle. "What man does to the Earth he does to himself. If you spit on the earth, you spit on yourself".

III. *It is spiritually alive.* It maintains that spirituality is of inherent importance to the human condition. Yet it suggests, at the same time, that traditional spiritualities are no longer adequate. We need a form of spirituality which simultaneously heals the earth and heals our inner selves.

IV. It starts from a single premis that *the world is a sanctuary*. And from this premise it derives the whole web of concepts and values which are connected, coherent and rationality justified; and which consist of a sufficient basis for new tactics for living. Among the eco-values the chief are : reverence, responsibility, frugality and justice for all.

V. *It does not shy away from practical problems*. It realises that many of our actions misfire and lead to ecologically and socially unacceptable and even disasterous consequences because they are based on values which are skewed. By relating values to action, and by clearly seeing which forms of development are desireable and which are not, Eco-philosophy partakes in the economic debate by postulating that sustainable development must be:

a) ecologically responsible;
b) economically viable;
c) life-enhancing;
d) culturally sensitive.

In brief, the world as a sanctuary is an expression of an old idea. But in our day and age it has a new meaning. It actively invites us to make the world one enormous sanctuary. It invites us to undertake a new kind of responsibility, which is ecological responsibility. This responsibility is an important part of spiritual work for our times. It also invites us to take responsibility for future generations.

Spirituality and God are not abstract realms to which we aspire in our moments of meditation. We are called to make the world divine and sacred because we are not mere spectators in it. We are divine intelligences participating in the divine cosmos. We have to simultaneously keep the inner temple and the outer temple clean. We can't escape into the garden of our inner serenity, while the world becomes one toxic dump. The new ecological dance of Shiva is one in which we must participate. For this is the dance of our sanity, of our spirituality, of our strength, of our co-creating with the universe which brought us here with the purpose to make this world more divine.

Chapter 8

On Ethics and the High Road

The Pecularity of Ethics

Human beings are peculiar animals. They create for themselves so many difficulties, blocks, obstacles. One of them is ethics and the moral demands which society puts on us. Just think how lovely it would have been if there were no restraints; if you could do just as you please, without anybody making any fuss whatsoever. Think further, how lovely it would have been if there were no laws — you could be a god upon yourself.

Except that it would be not so lovely. More likely than becoming gods, human beings would have become beasts, and before you would have had a chance of being a god upon yourself, you would have been torn apart by the marauding human wolves.

Thus the law is for a purpose. And ethics is for a purpose. But the purpose of each is different. While obeying the law keeps you out of prison, following the moral law is a form of liberation and ultimately a road to heaven. Yes, this is what ethics is, that is, at its best, when it spells out the high road of human destiny. Ethics has been invented to point out the high road — as difficult as it is — to make you actualize your deepest self, to make you yearn for the stars. You do not have to reach for the stars. You do not have to follow the high road. But if you don't you are less than human.

Ethics is an extraordinary subject. Its purpose is to help the human. Yet it behaves as if it wanted to constrain the human, to put him in bondage; sometimes it appears as if ethics wanted to crucify the human, or at least make us miserable with its endless prohibitions. On the surface of it, it would appear that, if the purpose of ethics is to make us happy, it should be more indulgent. Yet, this is not how it works in human life. Indulgence is not the key of happiness. Indulgence is the road of unhappiness.

Ethics follows a different route. It proposes that life needs structure and proper constraints. And that human life flourishes amidst exacting and beautiful constraints. Life, like a sculptor, chisels out of the evolutionary flow forms of exquisite beauty amidst extraordinary constraints. Seen in the evolutionary perspective, ethics is a sculptor carving out the human material statues of enduring beauty, dignity, courage, radiance. Ethics is this challenger which forces individual human beings and tells them: "Now you dare to make out of your life something great and enduring in spite of the frailty of human nature and in spite of all the temptations of the world." I take exception here to the statement of Immanual Kant, so often repeated by Sir Isaiah Berlin, that out of the crooked timber of humanity no straight things can be made. This is a misconception.

Understanding proper constraints is all important. If the constraints are too crushing, we break up and become amorphous. We, therefore, should talk about beautiful constraints, these tests of life which elicit the best and the most noble out of us, in the service of life, God, and other human beings. This is what ethics has been at its best – a messenger of human greatness, dignity and courage. This courage and dignity are achieved through hard work, through discipline, sometimes through suffering and self-sacrifice.

Why have we developed so many ethics? Why so many moralities? Why the conflicts among them? Why our moral confusion? If life needed a strong and exacting system of constraints to give us a right support and a right structure, why not one good ethical system? Because this is not how life works. Life works through continuous and relentless unfolding. The result of this unfolding is the relentless process of articulation. Because life is so diverse and relentlessly articulating itself, *it flowers in ever new forms.*

The diverse systems of ethics in human cultures represent the articulation of life in ethical and aesthetic forms. When we look at the variety of ethics and their often incompatible character from a superficial perspective, the impression may be formed that they are whimsical and subjective entities. A deeper evolutionary perspective informs us that it is not so. All the diverse systems of ethics are the relentless responses of life to new circumstances. *As human life seeks new forms, it also articulates itself in new ethical imperatives.*

There is nothing subjective in the process. As there is nothing subjective in the unfoldment of evolution. At one time evolution attempted to articulate itself through *absolute ethical laws* and imperatives which were usually pronounced through the authority of god(s) and religions. This worked but only for a limited period of history. Then these absolutes were felt as unbearable constraining and suffocating dogmas.

At other times, human societies tried to live on the basis of complete relativism. But these were found unsatisfactory as well. Life needs supports and constraints. Ethical nihilism and relativism do not provide good moral supports. So life searches on, to find the most enduring, flexible and supportive forms, through which the effervescent of the human spirit can be expressed. In recent times, Life has created Eco-Ethics.

The High Road

What are values? Commands from heaven. Even if they were not, they should be treated as such. Whose heaven? Our joint common heaven: the world conceived of as a place of peace, justice, dignity, beauty and happiness.

Pigs do not need values. Neither do we — if we agree to live in a pigstay. Criminals, pathological killers and people without any sense of good and evil do not need values — as they live mindlessely and sometimes kill others mindlessly.

Only we need values, we the human beings who uphold a sense of sancity of life, who believe in the beauty and dignity of life, and who aspire to make life beautiful and dignified. Values were thus invented for those who have high regard for life, who, in a sense, conceive of life as a gift of heaven. In this sense values are commands from heaven — attributes of our thinking and behaviour which bring us closer to heaven.

On one point there can be no disagreement: values are these vehicles, these modes of our being and forms of behaviour which make us supremely human; not just ordinarily human. For our ordinary humanity so easily slides into a behaviour characteristic of the pigstay. *Only when we try to be supremely human, we become human*. Such is our predicament — and such is our road.

The problem with values — religious, ethical, social, existential — begins when we start to articulate the idea of heaven, the idea of the human, the idea of justice, dignity, sanctity of life. Although the interpretations of these ideas are many, and sometimes they clash with each other, this should not prevent us from pursuing the High Road of our humanity.

To sceptics and cynics, we shall respond from the outset: no, it is not the case that everything is relative. There is a life of dignity, beauty, justice and freedom, on the one hand, and there is humdrum, undisciplined, sloppy, irresponsible existence, on the other hand. The former requires high values and is an embodiement of high values. The latter is a renunciation of high values — as it represents this variant of the human condition which is much below our possibilities. So the discourse on values begins with the question: what kind of human do you want to be and do you think you deserve to be?

The literature on the subject of values is enormous. It is expressed in religious books, in philosophical treatises, in dramas and novels, in essays and editorials. Almost everybody is vying for your soul. Yes, to *influence and control your values is to possess your soul*. Beware of that.

In the West the most articulate positions on the subject of values are expressed in books on ethics, such as *Nichomachean Ethics,* by Aristole, or *Ethics,* by Spinoza. These are the treatises showing us the High Road. Much can be learnt about human nature by studying these treatises.

In India the most valuable discourses on values can be found in such sacred traditional books as the *Upanishads* and *Bhagavad Gita*. These books are still the source of moral guidance in people's lives. Again, these books outline the High Road of humanity.

The old venerable books on values give us a map of how human beings have struggled with their own nature and their own distiny. Yet with each new epoch, new problems arise and new threats appear to our integrity, to our quest for beauty, to our striving for dignity and divinity. In our times the threats to our identity, to our dignity, to our well being have been numerous. We need to recognize them and find appropriate moral responses. For if we don't, we drift; and end up in confusion, incoherence and meaninglessness. We abandon the High Road for a confusing one. The older moral and ethical strategies for safeguarding our integrity are still valid in many ways. However in our times new moral insights and strategies must be found to cope with new threats. Of these new insights I will concentrate on the following three:

1. Don't be too easily persuaded that you amount to nothing. You are a glorious star of God's horizon.
2. Don't allow yourself to be easily manipulated for the benefit of some and at the expense of many others. Your quest is one of universal justice and fairness.
3. Don't allow yourself to be used for the schemes which work to the detriment of other humans, of non-human beings, and of nature. Your duty is to encourage and enhance inter-species solidarity and the well being of all beings.

The above precepts follow from one idea, that of the sanctity of life. You need to remember: if sanctity of life is not upheld, only chaos, confusion and disintegration can result.

Resist the Forces of Expedience

You may now wonder why do we witness many new threats to human dignity and human sovereignty in the world, which, we were told, was becoming more and more civilized? Perhaps we should make a clarification by noticing that the ever-growing development of civilization does not make society ever-more civilized. Something has happened in the way our civilization has developed. The promise of the civilized life in the wake of powerful forces of civilization has not been fulfilled. On the contrary, by some kind of strange dialectics, the powerful unfolding of civilization has unleashed great forces of savagery.

The individual has been caught in the web of the powerful forces which civilization has developed. Science and technology at one time promised to be the liberators of humankind. Through their benefits, universal fulfilment and happiness were to encircle the earth. This has not happened. Instead the more powerful science and technology has become, the more clearly they attempted to subdue the individual to their cold rational schemes. The great philosopher Immanuel Kant (1728-1804) already perceived this danger as he saw that science was good at exploring the external world but mute about human freedom and human dignity. He, therefore, declared: "The starry heaven upon you and the moral law within you." This was a radical separation of science from morality. It was an explicit assertion that the laws of science govern the outside universe, while the moral universe of the human is governed by the inner imperative of human conscience. Hence "the moral law within you". Freedom and sovereignty of the individual are rooted in the moral conscience of the humans, which is outside the domain of science. Hence the conclusion: science must not meddle in our moral universe. We are the moral sovereigns upon ourselves.

The salutary teaching of Kant is still relevant for our times, particularly as science and technology, if only indirectly, have attempted to subdue and manipulate the human universe to the imperatives and schemes which have very little to do with human happiness and liberation; and have much to do with greed, profit, expansion, control and manipulation. In these schemes of control and manipulation, the individual is so often reduced to a pawn, to a cipher, to a nothing. As the result of the unrestrained reign of science and technology, we have witnessed a thoroughgoing process of *reduction* of the human to cogs and wheels, whereby the individual is deprived of freedom, dignity and sovereignty.

Thus it is extremely important for you personally not to be too easily persuaded that you amount to nothing. You are a very wonderful creation of the universe. Thus fight for your dignity, freedom and sovereignty. There have always been forces in human society which attempted to level down the individual. But these forces have never been so numerous and so powerful as in the technological society.

The second precept which I stated was as follows: don't allow yourself to be manipulated for the benefit of the powerful rich and at the expense of the dispossessed poor. The difference in status, power and wealth has always been a fact of life. But nowadays we confront a new phenomenon. After centuries and millennia of the gradual disapperance of outragious inequities, during which we have consciously and deliberately promoted equity and justice among people — we are now witnessing sinister attempts to reverse this historical process. Through some clever, if not diabolical schemes, during the last decades or so, the rich have become richer and the poor poorer. This is most strange and unjust. This, in fact, flies into the face of the idea of justice, morality, humanity. As this gap between the rich and the poor increases, we observe great suffering and anguish. The progress of the rich is marked by the blood of the poor. This whole new development is unholy, immoral and it must be resisted. Otherwise, the growing process of injustice will result in bloddy upheavals by the poor. The five per cent of the privileged cannot be the rulers of the planet. For this is against democracy, against justice, against God's plan.

The third precept which I stated asserted: don't allow yourself to be used for the destruction of nature. Don't align yourself with any schemes or practices which lead to the needless destruction of the fragile cycles of nature. Let us be aware, we have always harvested and used nature to our advantage. What we have witnessed in our times is the wholesale destruction of nature; also the accelerated destruction of species. Remember, once you eliminate a given species, even God cannot return it back to existence.

The protection of nature — as our Mother, as our habitat, as our sustenance — is enormously important, and it is now our new moral imperative. In olden days people lived in natural harmony with nature, woven into its cycles. There was no need to exhort humans to protect nature for it was their outer skin, so close to them that they would not dream of mutilating it. Besides, they had not the means to do so.

Then the humans separated themselves from nature and sought their freedom through subduing nature and through the manipulation of the external world. The exploitation of nature — to man's advantage and the manipulation and control of the external world became the *unwritten moral commandments of the post-Renaissance man*. These commandments have become ingrained on the technological consciousness of 20th century people. The grip of these commandments is still powerful, in spite of the fact that we now clearly see what havoc we have brought upon nature. It is thus important to announce the protection of nature as our new moral imperative.

The main conclusions of our discourse, so far, are as follows:

— resist reduction of your humanity to the stuff of the machine;

— resist the spread of injustice-remembering that we are one human family, united by the bond of solidarity;

— resist the destruction of nature-remembering that you are one of its branches.

The problems I have discussed are not typical moral problems which one finds in traditional books and precepts. Rather they are new moral problems of our times. For this reason they are not addressed in the traditional literature. And precisely for this reason they must be addressed and articulated — for we do not find guidance with regard to these problems in traditional ethics and morality. Among these problems the protection of nature (and the protection of our life and of future generations) looms very large. Protection of nature, when seriously conceived, leads to a host of new strategies and indeed the idea of ecological ethics.

Eco-Ethics as an Expression of the High Road

I have written on ecological ethics, and on eco-values, in my earlier publications (see especially *Dancing Shiva in the Ecological Age*, New Delhi, 1995). In this essay I simply want to emphasize that the protection of nature cannot be a pious wishful-thinking activity, whereby we wish that other people should be less destructive of nature. Nor can it be merely a vigorous action of young activists, who want to protect a given river bed or even the whole range of the Himalayas. It must be a *metaonia,* turning things inside out, establishing a new relationship with nature and with ourselves — but on a deep metaphyscial level, and not through superficial exhortations: "let us save nature."

This new attitude to nature must be based on a new image of the world. We must view the *universe as a sanctuary;* not as a machine. In this sanctuary we need to behave as shepherds and as custodians. Some would even want to say as priests — reverentially and with deep respect to our sanctuary. Thus reverence for life and for our sanctuary/earth emerges as the basic ecological value. From this value immediately follows the second major value: *responsibility as reverence in action*.

The third major ecological value is *frugality, conceived as grace without waste*. Frugality, within our fragile planet, is so important that we need to elevate it to a moral virtue. Thus remember, you vote most importantly through your lifestyles — elegantly frugal or horrendously wasteful.

Now I am not saying that saving a river bed, and especially the Himalaya, through concerned actions is not important. But I am saying that this action must be accompanied by a new consciousness and new values (of reverence for life, of responsibility, of frugality). When we possess this new consciousness and are guided by new values, then we go into action with a new purpose and energy. Our action is then more rooted, more convincing and has better chances to succeed. Ultimately, we need to spread our new consciousness and our new values so that there is no necessity to fight for every threatened habitat — as we shall be guided by reverence and not greed.

The main battle for preserving the earth and for maintaining a meaningful future will be a moral one. This is one of the main points of my discourse.

One of the practical extensions of eco-ethics is the idea of sustainable development, which is an umbrella concept containing a number of strategies, policy recommendations and also moral values. This idea was born in the 1980s when negative consequences of rampant technology, serving traditional development, became obvious. To be truly and genuinely sustainable, any development, in my opinion, should be:

— Ecologically responsible
— Economically viable
— Socially equitable, and
— Culturally sensitive or culture-specific.

Any development which makes sense in the long run must be ecologically responsible. For if it leads to ecological ruin, what we witness is a process of ruination, not development.

Genuine development must be economically viable. It must be self-supporting in the long run. Yet this viability must be accountable not only in economic terms but simultaneously in social and ecological terms. If ecological consequences are neglected, we are back to the situation of the ecological ruination. Any development must be a rational enterprise. A form of development which leads to stupid ruinous consequences is not rational.

Meaningful and worthy development must be just and equitable. It must benefit not just the privileged individuals or societies which manipulate the whole process of development but local people, a vast majority of them. Sustainable development must fulfill the promise which material progress failed to deliver. It must be the vehicle of social and human amelioration. But it must not concentrate on one aspect of the human existence — the material well being. It must address itself to the entire human condition, including its phychological, social and spiritual aspects. Otherwise, it will become a failure, as material progress has already become. The possibility of this failure is lurking behind as too many people think of development, including sustainable development, in material terms alone.

Sustainable development should be culture specific, sensitive to the conditions of the culture in which it takes place. Let us express this idea in stronger terms. *There isn't one universal model of development which is "best" for all environmental and cultural conditions.* Classical economics has laboured under the illusion that there is one universally valid economic knowledge — for all human cultures and circumstances. The truth is that each culture needs a model of development which is suitable to its history and its characteristics. Only such a model, which is very sensitive to the cultural milieu, can succeed as a truly sustainable model.

Seen from a larger perspective, sustainable development implies sustainable lifestyles and sustainable values, which we cherish and want to prepetuate. The three realms co-define and support each other, they are a trinity within the unity.

Each side of the triangle implies the other two. Sustainable development will not be possible if it is accompanied by wasteful lifestyles and purely materialist values of consumption. We live

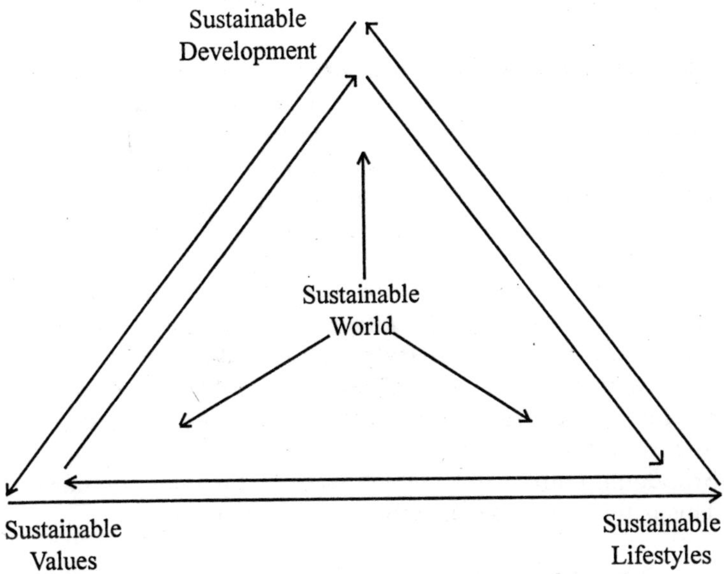

a unitary world to such a degree that it almost boggles our mind.

The ethics of solidarity, participation, empathy and compassion which the conception of the new sustainable world requires, only echoes ancient teachings, namely, that all people are one, all the world is one, and that we must live in peace in order to survive and in order to enter the High Road which ultimately leads to liberation, self-actualization and happiness.

Chapter 9

The Meaning of Politics in a Spiritual Perspective

The Art of Good Government

Political institutions are a shadow of our souls. Put otherwise, political institutions express and embody the wisdom of the people of the time. If there is no such wisdom among the people, these institutions express their unwidsom. The state of our wisdom and the state of our soul are closely related.

Our institutions do not work because our souls do not work. Our spiritual blight affects our individual lives and our institutions alike. Let us state it clearly. We cannot have good political institutions if our visions are cripplingly narrow and our wisdom lamentably limited. Thus, the road to good political and social institutions is by deepening our wisdom and by broadening our visions: which is to say by enlarging our souls. This is the only way. And there is no other way.

Our technology is stupendous. Our technical instruments often dazzle in their capacity to perform. However, our political institutions cannot be conceived of as merely technical instruments. Perfect technical instruments are often perfectly insensitive to the human needs and desiderata. Wise politics needs much more than good technical tools. It needs empathy and deep understanding of our inner longings.

What is then the right recipe for building a political system or for reconstructing a political system? Do not concentrate on merely reforming the institutions, especially by trying to make them into "perfect" technical instruments. Acquire wisdom. Mend and enlarge your visions. Go deeper into yourself. Then your institutions will work. And only then.

Yet, here is the rub. It is one of the most difficult things for any people, to admit that their institutions do not work because of the smallness of their souls. For institutions are most of the time conceived as being "out there", as instruments regardless of who we are. Yet, we must remember: these institutions are a shadow of who we are.

We blame our institutions for our plight, for our dissatisfaction, for our unhappiness. Why? Because it is very hard for us to admit that we have the institutions we deserve, that we are responsible for these institutions, that they reflect our inner selves, that is to say, our inner worth. I am aware that the kind of statements I make are not welcome. Often they are ignored as annoying. Why? Because they pose too much challenge to ourselves. Yet, if these statements reveal the truth, then the conclusion is: don't blame institutions for what they are. Blame yourself for who you are. And don't hide. Hiding accomplishes nothing. Are you prepared to change yourself? No. So, don't expect the institutions to change. The institutions only reflect who you are, including your indolence, your lack of responsibility, your "*manana*" attitude, your waiting for "Godot".

Don't expect politicans and even political scientists to help you, for they are completely conditioned by the past and possessed by the collective unwisdom of our time. They cultivate your smallness. They think that by putting you into the cast of your smallness, you are comfortable there. Deep down you are not. Let us call the poet Goethe as our witness. He said :

To treat man as he is
Is to debase him.
To treat man as he ought to be
Is to engrace him.

Politicians and social scientists want to treat us as we are, constantly reducing us in our stature and possibilities. We know that we are pretty low in our lowest aspects. But this is not the ground for celebrating our humanity. We celebrate our humanity by aspiring to what is best in us, by attempting to become what we can potentially become, what we ought to be in the best sense of the term. Only then we enshrine our deepest humanity, give a testimony to who we truly are.

Social scientists are obsessed nowadays with measuring. But what do they measure? To measure empirically our unwisdom, as expressed through our consumptive attitudes, is not a scientific confirmation of who we are. It is rather a sad capitulation of the scientific mind to the lower realm of human possibilities.

When they work to our advantage, political institutions must lead the people, must be like great religious symbols to which we aspire. And while aspiring to them, we change ourselves in the process. It is thus clear that political institutions must not follow the people, especially, if by following the people, we mean reducing the people to their lower selves. For it does not help much if we create political institutions in the image of reduced people.

To break this vicious cycle we need to ascend to a higher perspective, to a spiritual perspective from which we can see things more clearly and with a greater depth and understanding. Thus, we need to see that satisfaction and happiness also mean the inner peace and the nourishment of the soul. Some are allergic to the term "soul". Let us not be led astray by words. We are simply saying that there is inside of us this human core which is trans-physical and trans-biological. It has its needs and demands, the satisfaction of which as indispensable to the meaning of our life as the oxygen is to our lungs. We know this truth well.

Now, this human core, which has traditionally been called soul, is something without which our uniquely human life withers. Social and political institutions must safeguard all aspects of our being. If social and political institutions neglect our inner lives, or are in collision with our inner selves, then we whither. Such institutions are not worthy of our support and allegiance.

I need not belabour the fact of the plight of present political and social institutions (particularly in the developed world) in providing the shelter for our spiritual life. To respond that these institutions are secular in character and that we live in a secular society is to obviate my argument and not to meet it. It is so, for two reasons. One is that our spiritual or inner life must not be confined to the religious life and religious institutions. The separation of the state from the church, of our civic institutions from our religious institutions, does not mean neglecting and eliminating our inner lives, our spiritual quests, our inner core. Spirituality and religion must not be confused with each otheror conflated with one another. To gaze at the stars and to see in them an immense temple does not require priests, church, or religion.

The second reason is even more important. The so-called secular society, delivered on the wheels of material progress may not be much of a society, if by "society" we mean such an arrangement of human life through which this life is enhanced and not dwarfed. If by the secular society we mean one in which "*homo homini lupus est*" (man is wolf to a man); in which we witness the growing violence on the streets, and in the family, in which we witness the growing injustice, as the poor become poorer and more dispossessed, then we might want to take a deep breath, pause for a while and ask: might it all not be a manifestation of the sickness of our soul? If our reason continuously deceives us and leads us astray, then we need to go deeper — to the structure of our wisdom and the state of our soul. For not infrequently our deeper maladies have their source there.

We are so used to the idea that politics is the arena for the selfish, greedy, and rapacious, that we tend to forget and disregard the examples that prove just the opposite. These examples which show that politics is for the noble, selfless, high minded, and idealistic are numerous. There is much we can learn from these examples, if we choose to. More important still, they show that the politics as the exercise of the power of the soul is possible and that when it is practised thus, it brings about remarkable and positive results.

Confucius

In ancient times in China there lived a sage Kung-Fu-Tse, whose name has been simplified in the West as Confucius (551-479 B.C.). He was renowned for his sagacity, wisdom, impartiality, justice, and the capacity to see through the distant consequences of human actions. In due time he was invited by the king of Lu province to govern the kingdom. And he ruled for twelve years with the blessing of the king and the growing happiness of the people, showing what wisdom can do when consistently applied in social-political affairs. Confucius' rule was so successful, while the prosperity and peace of the people in the kingdom was growing, that the neighbouring kingdoms were astounded and became envious. This was a clear demonstration that politics could be a noble and beautiful art benefitting all.

Then one of the neighbouring kings somehow bribed the king of Lu, who Confucius worked for, and suggested that Confucius should be sent for a holiday for one year. So he went for a holiday. He was not assassinated nor did he die in ignominy. But he never returned to rule again, though he wanted to.

For Confucius the ideal consists of the harmony between the superior individual and a well ordered society, which is based on the mutual moral obligations of the five basic human relationships between: ruler and minister, father and son, elder brother and younger brother, husband and wife and one friend to another. Government is to be conducted through the ruler's moral example. The difference between the mature man, whom Confucius calls a superior man and an immature man, whom he calls an inferior man, is that for the former the rule is moral principle.

One of the conclusions is that we need to mature spiritually to produce such people as Confucius and then we need to allow them to show us what the art of government is about. For what is going on with present governments is not so much that they are led by unwise and often selfish people (which is undoubtedly true) but that the people who elected them are unwise not to know and not to demand any better.

Confucious' teaching has survived over two millennia and is still inspiring people. It does not really matter that Confucius was Chinese and his teaching may be more resonant with the Chinese psyche than the Western one. What matters is that he is a shining example of a philosopher who built his philosophy on spiritual principles and yet was capable of applying this philosophy to practical and political affairs with such success that he can truly be called a philosopher King.

We should not conclude too rashly that the political influence of Confucius ceased with his death. It still continues. Nowadays some Asian nations, after tiring of American domination and Western decadence, which is imposed on them as modernity, return to the Confucian teaching in order to combat what they consider as an ideological imperialism. In places like

Singapore, but not only, the respect for the traditional Confucian values is said to be the backbone of the social cohesion as contrasted with Western alienation and disintegration. Thus, the political legacy of Confucius lives on and is seen as remarkably sustainable. Why? Because it is based on something deeper than the expedient values of political manipulation.

Ashoka

Ashoka was an Indian king who ruled in the third century B.C. (269-232). He was a man endowed with extraordinary strength and physical and spiritual powers. Through his military genius and extraordinary physical prowess, he conquered all the neighbouring kingdoms and truly unified India at the time. And then one day, after a huge battle, seeing the rivers of blood running in front of him, he woke and decided that this was not the way. He became a follower of the Buddhist creed of compassion and non-violence. He did not relinquish his kingdom. He did not run to a cave in the mountains to repent. Instead he ruled as a spiritual monarch. And remarkable indeed was his rule and his achievement.

First he built 84,000 stupas (Buddhist monument/chapels) in all the villages and towns of India. Each of them was a visible commandment that compassion, social justice, and non-violence were to be the foundation of society. Then he carved in rock his famous edicts proclaiming that social and political life was to based on the spiritual foundations of justice and compassion. Only in the nineteenth century did we start to rediscover the famous Ashoka edicts. So far, we have found over forty of them. How many are still buried in the jungles or under the mounds of earth we do not know. But what we did discover is impressive enough! The rocks carved by Ashoka's messengers are as far apart as Pakistan and Burma, some two and one half thousand kilometres. Communication and transport were not easy at the time; they are still not easy on the Indian subcontinent. Yet, with remarkable will and persistance, Ashoka wielded his vast empire into a political organism based on Buddhist philosophy.

He did not create a religious state run by the monks, although he sometimes considered himself a Buddhist monk. He was a truly enlightened monarch. He ruled single handedly through his various emissaries who ran from one end of his empire to another carrying his messages and overseeing that justice and non-violence were observed. Though Buddhist to the core, the language of his messages, and of his edicts, were often not explicitly Buddhist. The country was still dominated by the Hindu Brahmins, particularly in remote villages and these were not to be antagonized. Yet, Ashoka did more in spreading Buddhism throughout the Indian sub-continent than all the Buddhist monks taken together.

The remarkable thing is that Ashoka's purpose was not to be a religious missionary. His purpose was to establish good law, or to be more explicit, good Dharma. This Dharma was for the benefit of all, not for one caste or another. In Ashoka's case we witness a unique situation (within the Indian spiritual tradition whereby the moral law, Good Dharma, is announciated *for all regardless of caste*. It was Dharma based on universal justice - the foundation of just and equal society.

Ashoka's case (and also the one of Confucius) is more telling and more paradigmatic than we are usually aware. It is simply not the case that these were two wise men who stumbled upon good principles which helped them to rule. The spiritual principles and good government are part and parcel of each other. As the spiritual awareness spread and became accepted by the populace, good government became possible and indeed inevitable. Here is an important conclusion: the art of government for the people and with the people is possible when people become aware of deeper spiritual principles underlying all life and the forms of sustaining government.

Ecology as a Commitment to the Sanctity of Life

The discussion of environmentalism is acquiring a new dimension. It is ultimately right and proper to ask whether our environmental concerns have a religious bearing, and if so, what is the nature of the spiritual and religious commitment environmentalism implies.

The idea of the sacredness of the web of life has religious undertones. We need to recognise it, and perhaps even cherish it. In our confused age, plagued by the meaninglessness of life and the atrophy of values, would it be such a terrible thing to give our allegiance to the Earth — and therefore to life itself —

by rallying behind ecology and by considering environmentalism a sacred project which unites us all? Whatever our race and religion, ecology binds us all together. In this sense, ecology is the universal religious project of our time.

Life without commitment is an empty and futile life. A deep commitment ultimately means a spiritual commitment, a form of religious commitment. Is your life to be fulfilled by your commitment to consumption alone? Or do you need something deeper to feel truly human? Isn't a commitment to environmentalism a commitment to sanity, a commitment to your children and grandchildren, a commitment to the sanctity of life? If this is to be called a religion, it is surely one that we can all afford.

Green Politics Must Be Based on a Vision

Why is the political life of so-called major democracies so drab, so uninspiring? Why are the politicians so small and so unable to lead? Why is there no vision and no imagination in the social realm? Has the human race become so dim that it no longer produces capable people?

The answers to our seemingly *political* questions is outside politics, actually in the realm of religion. The roots, of our problems lie in our shallow eschatology. In the socio-political climate in which great human ideals are derided as unreal, as not pragmatic enough, potential political *leaders* are cut to size. They are forced to think small, to be manipulators because the whole culture thinks small and is essentially a manipulative culture.

Thus inadvertently, we produce midgets as part of the design of the consumptive materialist culture. This culture does not want to be challenged in its pedestrian, trivial pursuits. They very idea of the greatness of man clashes with the mundane ethos of the consumptive culture. Hence the unprecedented mediocracy in the present political life.

But green politics must not allow itself to be sucked into this consumptive vacuum. Politicians of green parties must realise that their mandate is to defend the glory of creation and the integrity of the earth. Therefore high ideals are an essential part of their belief. They must not allow themselves to be dragged to the level of present day small politicking. If they do, then this spells out a kiss of death for the green vision. Green politicians are not elected to parliments on the green ticket in order "to be there". They are elected to safeguard the integrity and the well-being of the earth through parliamentary means.

Green politicians should not shun sharing their vision with ordinary people for fear of being too idealistic. Ordinary people need vision and inspiration; they are starved of worth while ideals. After all, green politics is based on a vision, the vision of a clean healthy earth, capable of renewing itself and supporting many generations to come. The Dharma of green politics is to save the world, to make it blossom; and to make all creation blossom.

Chapter 10

To Understand Right is to Live Right

Life Requires Coherence

"I curse you to live at the time of change," so says an ancient Chinese proverb. We have been living during the time of enormous and epochal changes for quite a while. As the result of these changes in our outlooks, so many of our previously accepted beliefs simply collapsed, not only in the realm of religion but also with regard to science. The foundations of classical physics started to crumble at the beginning of the 20th century. At the end of the 20th century the whole edifice has been in pieces. Doubt and chaos started to prevail in Academia, in society and in our minds. The conviction has spread that all past beliefs and dogmas are gone. There is nothing we can believe in with any certainty. What is left is doubt, chaos and subjectivity.

This is the scene against which to view the appearance of a new outlook called post modernism, which accepts present disintegration, and in a strange sense celebrates it, by proclaiming that "anything goes." On the surface of it, this is a liberating attitude, but impossible to maintain in actual human lives.

We cannot live our lives in chaos and confusion because life requires coherence. We cannot accept the idea "anything goes" (which post modernism advocates) for it can lead to the kind of nihilism that is lethal. We simply cannot allow the individuals who want to destroy nature and pollute the environment to do so, even if such is their desire. Even less can we allow the individuals who have sadistic tendencies to harm other people or to kill them for sports. Thus it is clear that not "anything goes."

While maintaining the stance, "we cannot allow", I am not in favour of authoritarian solutions: to impose draconian laws from above and to force people to some prearranged coherence. No. I am advocating something else: a deeper understanding of who we are, where we are, and where we are going. Instead of a lazy attitude " It is all in pieces, let us enjoy the choas", I am proposing that we must bring from within ourselves new resources of knowledge and of imagination — to bring the world to a new coherence within which our lives will be meaningful, connected, and even radiant. Yes, such a thing is possible. To understand right is to live right. We don't life right because we do not understand right. In most general terms, we are talking here about the Dharma of right understanding.

We must not be confused about fundamental things. There is LIFE. Life has meaning. Moreover, life is sacred. Deep down we all recognize the sanctity of life. This awareness is smoldering in each of us — namely that the spark of life is the most precious thing that we all have. The phenomenon of life, in each of us individually and in all individuals outside ourselves, when approached aright, reveals itself to be such an extraordinary, awesome and fantastic happening, that a true understanding of it naturally and inevitably leads to reverence for it. *Thus, the sanctity of life reveals itself as a part of our deeper understanding of it.*

The time has come to give up old metaphors. Instead of thinking of the universe as a huge clock-like mechanism, and consequently of binding ourselves in all kinds of crippling deterministic epicycles, we need to think of the universe in an altogether different way. How? *The World is a Sanctuary.*

In recreating the world, we need to start with cosmology, or our world view. From the idea of the world as a sanctuary, the sanctity of life follows naturally. To fully comprehend the world as a sanctuary is to revere it, is to treat life as sacred. If we do not do so, we do not understand the meaning of the sanctuary. Indeed many ancient cultures understood this fundamental point quite clearly as they declared both the cosmos and life in it as sacred, special, exquisite. This assumption is much more palatable to human reason than the assumption that the world is a senseless mechanistic aggregate of physical bits of matter.

Let us observe that we now have the foundations for a new ethics. From the idea of the world as a sanctuary follows *reverence for life* as the main ethical imperative. If the world is a sanctuary then reverence for all there is, is an inevitable consequence. *Thus from an intelligent reading of the cosmos implicitly follows Eco-ethics*. We need to explicate its features.

From reverence for life naturally follows *responsibility* — as the second major value of eco-ethics, the responsibility for your own life, for the well being of nature, for future generations, for everything there is. *Responsibility is reverence in action*. You cannot be truly reverential unless you exercise your responsibility — for the sanctuary and for everything there is in it. This sense of responsibility is empowering. It gives us wings and an enormous mandate for the future: we are here as the custodians, responsible guardians of all the heritage of life.

From responsibility there follows the third ecological value — *frugality*. Frugality should be defined as *grace without waste,* as doing more with less, as treading gently on the earth. In other words, responsibility must be translated into appropriate life styles, life styles which are gentle and unharmful to nature and other beings. *Frugality is both an ethical imperative and a political one*. We vote most eloquently with our life styles. If our life styles cause stress and injustices to other parts of the world, then obviously we are not being responsible, nor are we reverential to all life on earth.

We need to have the courage of our mind in elucidating and expressing the things which we feel and know in our instincts. Why do we identify with ecology? What is so important in understanding it in depth? An in-depth comprehension of ecology is reverence in action, is a deep identification with the beauty of life pulsating through the universe until we become part of it. Thus understanding becomes empathy. Empathy becomes universal reverence. This reverence is a form of spirituality. *In our times the ecological and the spiritual become one*. The Dharma of right understanding is powerful.

Fly in Control

This new perspective, which I call the ecological world view, spells out a new freedom for humans. We are doomed to freedom! We have the freedom of imaginatively co-creating with God. We must claim this new freedom, otherwise we shall disintegrate into the miasma of destructive epicycles, decomposing oursevles. We have the mandate for the *freedom to fly*. But we must fly in control. No more anchors and dogmas but flying in control. Such is our destiny. This requires courage, as well as a strong sense of belonging to this world, as well as the will to participate in the fascinating cosmic journey. The terms "cosmic journey" should not frighten us. For we are cosmic beings. And we have a cosmic destiny.

Thus, the characteristics of the new human are courage, freedom, imagination, and the capacity to fly in control – without crashing like Icarus did. As a part of our equipment, we need prudence and wisdom, the attributes which ancient cultures understood and cultivated well. Yes, wisdom is possible and prudence is possible and we need to cultivate them in order to overcome the present paralysis and inertia. We also need to cultivate hope, which is spring everlasting. Without hope, life crumbles. Hope is an invisible scaffolding of all life and all human strivings.

The picture we have sketched above, we dare say, is more intelligent and coherent than present doom inspired writings of so-called post-modernists. They do not offer us any vision, but only the vistas of bleak despair. One lives by hope, not by despair.

The present crisis is a challenge to our imagination and courage. We must have this imagination and courage to build anew — positively and creatively. The ecological world view is one response to the challenge of our times. This world view is hilostic and connected not because it attempts to re-integrate the old scattered pieces. It is holistic and reverential through a new vision of the cosmos.

True Harmony Must Include Nature

Harmony of mind, body and soul, to which so many aspire, is a beautiful thing. It is a sure sign of human maturity. Yet when this harmony is only limited to the individual, it is an incomplete harmony and it leads to imperfect balance.

Real and all embracing harmony, which represents a holistic world view and a holistic life-style, requries and demands that we think of harmony in terms of : Body - Mind/Soul - Nature. Peace with nature and harmony with nature is an essential aspect of any meaningful harmony.

Spiritual seekers and even great accomplished masters do not understand that the essence of ecology is not cleaning the physically polluted environment, but something deeper - re-establishing the balance between the humans and Nature. This balance has been so badly strained that in order to regain it, which also means regaining our own equilibrium and balance, we need to do a major work of Catharsis. Otherwise our inner balance will be illusory. We have to simultaneously keep the inner and the outer temple clean. We cannot escape into the garden of our inner serenity, while the world becomes one toxic dump.

It is strange and really puzzling that after 25 years of continuous discussions about the importance of ecology, which above all signifies peace with nature, spiritually minded people are still unseeing. There seems to be a blind spot in their mind and hearts which prevents them from seeing that true harmony and inner balance must include Nature as part of our being.

The Vedas extol so beautifully and with such great reverence the beauty of Nature as we interact with her.

The dawn comes knocking at your door;
Arise, awake, 0 divine men,
The glorious sun has risen,
the radiant glow is flowing from the east,
dispersing the darkness of the night.
The new bright rays bring in renewed hope.
A new day is ushered in,
full of zest and zeal
and life progresses on its path of glory,
Each dawn brings a bright
ray of hope and a happy day.

(*Rig Veda*, 10.113.16)

Awake. Arise. Open your ecological eye. Open the space of your heart for all creatures and beings of Nature. This will be a testimony of your cosmic outreach. This will be evidence that you have arrived at a true and lasting harmony.

The light of understanding can be our saviour. But it must be deep understanding, not shallow understanding. Through shallow understanding, we have messed up the world. Through deep understanding, based on a cosmic vision of the world in which all beings are important in the evolutionary plan, we can regain the world and regain ourselves.

At the beginning was light. At the end there will be Ultimate Light. In between there is the Light of understanding - on which we flow and with which we shall reach Ultimate Light.

Chapter 11

The Yoga of the Himalayan Wonder

The Wonder

The Himalayas are the playground of Gods. If Gods did not exist, people gazing at the Himalayas would have been bound to invent them — such is the majesty, grandeur and power emanating from these peaks. What we become is brought out from within us through the interaction with the multitude of aspects of the external world. If we were eternally gazing at the landscape of the moon, our being would have become in the image of the monotonous lifeless scenery of the moon. The Himalayas, in contrast, present all the drama the human being can experience. The Himalayas themselves are the drama. From their explosive volcanic origins, through the storms and monsoons of the annual cycles, via the rolling hills with their exquisite flowers, rising to a tremendous crescendo of peaks reverbreating with an everlasting energy — the Himalayas offer every aspect of the drama known in human experience. Except that in the Himalayas it is all on the Himalayan scale.

There is something haunting and irresistable about the Himalayas. Like great spiritual ideals, they seem to be easily available - before you start reaching them. Like great spiritual ideals, they are always there, permanent, solid and shinning— no matter what.

Like no other mountains on this earth, like no other palce on this earth, the Himalayas belong to all humanity. Each of us has been personally tied to the Himalayas. For who of us has not dreamt about going there, and being there - if only for a while? Who of us has not been inspired and humbled by the Himalayan ethos — so overwhelming, so much beyond us, and so much calling us to measure ourselves against it?

Hence those celestial mountains serve as the ultimate point of reference of the greatness of our visions. We define ourselves and our projects in terms of their magnitude and grandeur. Our spiritual vision is helped and sustained by our awareness that they are there — pulling us upward, beyond our reach, but eternally calling us to their adobe. The spiritual journey is one in which one's grasp exceeds one's reach. And the Himalayas are the symbol of this reality which is continually beyond our reach but which continually we try to embrace.

What do the people do if they live in the shadows of the Himalayas, and do not want to be overwhelmed by them? They create philosophies of the Himalayan dimensions. Such is the story of the Vedic and Upanishadic traditions in ancient India. Living at the gates of the spectacular temple called the Himalayas, the ancient Hindus created the hymns and lithurgies of the splendour and magnitude of their enormous temple. Thus were created the most sublime and enduring texts that were ever conceived by the human mind.

Keep your graze fixed on the Himalayas and all your little worries will melt away. Keep your gaze fixed on the Himalayas and you will bathe in beauty. Keep your gaze fixed on the Himalayas and you will be closer to Gods. Keep your gaze fixed on the Himalayas and you will be closer to your inner self. The Himalayas are a symbol of our potential greatness and godliness. They are also a very potent symbol for our times. So many past religious symbols have crumbled, as they are unable to sustain us any more. The Himalayas stand up undiminished. They unite people of all religious denominations. They are one studpendous altar at which the earth sings the glory of creation. When you are close to the Himalayas you can hear their peaks singing amidst the total silence.

Of Temples and the Himalayas

Temples are great monuments which are a tribute to human imagination and prowess. They are awesome, beautiful and inspiring. In their lofty walls, you feel enlarged. While praying there, you grow in inner substance.

Yet there are also mountains. And there are the Himalayas. When I think of the Himalayas, a new scene of the grandeur and beauty opens in front of me. These craggy walls cascading with endless tapestry of snow and ice mosaics woven into each other are breathtaking. So dazzlingly white they are that you have to close your eyes at times. And then, in your mind, you see them even more resplendent. So vast they are that in order to reach their end, your eyes have to travel to heavens. What a piece of work of nature! What a majesty to behold!

I start praying. Yet, I don't know how to pray. Whether to sit in utter silence and meditate; or whether to dance with joy. Whether to submit in total humility; or whether to behave like a god brought to his true temple. You are so completely absorbed by the greatness and the glory of the Himalayas — you feel that you are nothing. At the same time, you are so ecstatically elevated by the sense of elation — you feel that you are everything. Oh, happy is the man who can experience the sense of nothingness and the sense of ultimate glory at the same time.

The Himalayas are so immovable, awesome and detached, yet so tender and inviting, ready to be your temple, your altar, your home. To enter them as a temple, you must come with appropriate reverence and awe. To pray at them as altars, you must liberate from yourself your inherent greatness. You do not need to evoke gods while being there. For you are among gods and deities. You are one of them.

The Himalayas bring out of us our utmost humility and our utmost sublimity. They release from within us our natural greatness while keeping our egos at bay. How can you not forget your ego when you are in the embrace of deities and gods?

If you gaze at the shining peaks of the Himalayas long enough, your mind will start shining with their glow.

Our delight with the Himalayas and our homage to all life is indeed part of the New Dharma — of the celebration of the greatness and sacredness of all there is.

Great and ravishing words were written in praise of the Himalayas. So much so that one is intimindated to say anything new. Yet we cannot just repeat the words of others. We have our own voice, our own heart, our own perception. We cannot be a generation which is mute. Therefore we must sing our own song.

Repeating the words of others, while our hearts are throbbing to sing to the Himalayas, would be a sign of spiritual atrophy. Every generation must discover its own Himalayas, must sing its own hymns to the Himalayas. Such is the nature of things.

The Himalayas want us to sing our own song to them. This is the way we become one with them. This is the way we deepen ourselves. To suppress our urge to sing to the Himalayas is suppressing our deepest nature.

To be ourselves, to do justice to our inner God, we need to stretch out our arms to heaven. Singing to the Himalayas is an expression of our arms embracing heaven. It is our existential necessity. It is our cosmic necessity.

If there is nothing you hold as sacred, there is no holiness within you. We need to enshrine the Himalayas in order to discover and manifest our own sacredness.

To experience the wonder of the Himalayas is to experience the wonder of your own being, is to experience the beauty resonating in your heart along with the grandeur resonating from the Himalayas. Great beauty is born of great experiences. The Himalayan miracle is a nurturer of our sense of beauty, of sublimity, of divinity.

Chapter 12

ECOLOGICAL SPIRITUALITY

Spirituality is a sublime subject. Great minds and souls have reflected on it and and left behind many illuminating insights. Yet we need to reflect on it again, if only because we wish to prove that we are spiritually alive. Our circumstances and problems are unprecedented and they require a new spiritual response, a new form of spirituality. Older spirtualities were created in response to different problems, within the context of a different world view, and in order to articulate different dimensions of the human condition.

Spirituality is an articulated essence of the human condition of a given time. This conception of spirituality enables us to cherish various forms of spirituality in various cultures and religions; but also informs us that there isn't one form of spirituality for all times, for all people, for all the conditions of the human universe. As the world changes and unfolds, knowledge grows and unfolds, the human mind changes, the human psyche changes, the human condition is re-articulated, and thus human spirituality takes different forms.

In our times we witness the dawn of the Ecological Perspective, or the ecological world view. Within this perspective the universe is viewed as a sanctuary. To act in the world as if it were a sanctuary is to make it reverential and sacred. What the universe becomes depends on you. Treat it like a machine and it becomes a machine. Treat it like a divine place and it becomes a divine place. Reverence for life, and for all there is in the universe, is the first condition of ecological spirituality. To celebrate the miracle of creation is to behold the world reverentially.

And in-depth comprehension of ecology is reverence in action, is a deep identification with the beauty of life pulsating through the universe until we become part of it. Thus understanding becomes empathy. Empathy becomes universal reverence. This reverence is a form of spiritually. *In our times the ecological and the spiritual become one.*

To worship God in our times is to save the planet. If we lose the environment, we lose God. Healing the planet and healing ourselves is spiritual work of the first mangitude in our day and age. Whatever our race and religion, ecology binds us all together. Ecology is the universal religious project of our time. The idea of redemption acquires a new meaning — it means redeeming the world by healing the earth. We need to emphasize: healing the earth is the spiritual work of our time.

To understand religious devotion is to recognize that all religions are forms of worship of the beauty and integrity of the planet. The greening of world religions in our times is a clear indication that the call of the crying earth is heard by the churches.

Spirituality is also, and has always been, the realization of our inner potential, the actualization of the inner god within us. We need to treat each other according to what we can potentially become: divine lights uplifting ourselves and helping others to heal, to integrate, to become more reverential. Working on ourselves to release and articulate our inner divinity and working in the outside world to heal the earth are complementary aspects of ecological spirituality.

The waning of religious forms of spirituality does not absolve us from the responsibility of healing the earth, and from actualizing our spiritual potential. In spite of the religious crisis of our times, and perhaps because of it, we must have the courage to meet — in each of us individually — not only the Jesus of Nazareth but the Messiah of the Cosmos.

Chapter 13

Some Consequences of Eco-Dharma

1. Live simply so that others may simply live.

2. Practice Frugality. Frugality is grace without waste.

3. Vote judiciously. We vote most eloquently with our lifestyles.

4. East simple food which is grown locally and which (preferably) is vegetarian.

5. Keep your confidence, keep believing in yourself, keep believing in the future.

6. As we are, so we think, so we behave — so we create the environment around ourselves. Purify yourself, keep clean within, create inner peace — then you will be capable to create right environments. The inner temple and the outer temple are aspects of each other.

7. Our Dharma has many aspects, many layers, many depths. In our times Dharma has been extended to include our care for Mother Earth. Eco-Dharma is a new blossoming of Dharma. Keep Eco-Dharma in your mind and heart all the time. Inspire others with this Dharma.

8. Your harmony with nature and other beings is a prerequisite for living sanely. Maintain this harmony. Develop right consciousness, which is holistic and ecological, based on compassion, cooperation, peace.

9. Walk in beauty. Embrace the Universe reverentially. This will lead you to a spiritual path. Following this path will lead you to genuine happiness.

10. The main aim of Eco-Dharma is to make ourselves sacred while taking all creation with us.

Chapter 14

Follow Your Own Nature

Follow your own nature... Your own deepest spiritual nature. Do not follow anybody else's nature. There are thousands of different flowers. Each blossoms differently. You have the right to blossom your own way.

We are all nourished by the same wonderful Mother Earth. We are all caressed by the same splendid sun. But the radiance of the sun is received and transformed in so many different ways. The spiritual light also can be received and transformed in so many different ways.

Find your own path. This path may already have a name. It may be called Taoist, Christian, Buddhist, Hindu, Muslim, Bahai. The name of the path is not important. Each of these paths is made of the eternal light of the universe - as received and transformed by various sages.

You are your own sage. You have the right to bask in the wisdom of the past. This is a gift of the universe given to each of us. You have the right to benefit from the enlightenment of past sages. They would be only too pleased if you do so.

Yet all the past enlightenment and all the past wisdom is but a reflection of the enormous light of the universe. You are part of the light of the universe. Shine your own light. The universe has made you in order that you can do so. For *you are a ray of light of the universe.*

Do not be afraid of your own light. Do not be afraid of yourself. There is a time to acknowledge that you are here to shine with the universe. If you are here not for this purpose, what purpose are you here for? You don't need to be arrogant about your own light. To acknowledge your own light is to acknowledge that the sun has blessed us all and that the universe is one miracle of light.

You are a small speck in the universe. But the light of the universe is within you. You need to transform this light according to your own nature. And then shine with your own light.

Chapter 15

VISION

What is a man's life without a vision? An empty shell reveberating with the sounds of others. If the eyes are given to us and never open, we are blind. If the gifts of vision and imagination are bestowed on us and we never use them, we grope in darkness. For life is as rich and extraordinary as we can imagine it to be. With no imagination, life is a tedious affair. Less than that. It becomes unbearable.

William Blake says:

> To the eye of the man of imagination
>
> Nature is Imagination itself.
>
> AS MAN IS, SO HE SEES.

And conversely, as man sees and imagines, so he is. The amoebas became eagles when they imagined themselves to be eagles. If this is a bit of an exaggeration, let it be so. But this exaggeration reveals an important truth, namely that what we think, what our vision imagines may become our reality. Our vision is a vehicle that leads us to the lands unknown, to the lands of beauty, to the lands of transcendence.

We do not live by vision alone. But without a vision we die a slow psychic death. We are nourished by bread, by soybeans, by the rays of sun. But equally we are nourished by the quality of our visions. A great vision is a thing of beauty that sustains us, makes life bearable and ultimately - radiant. Vision is not necessary for a hum-drum existence, only for a radiant one. Yet without vision even an ordinary existence is not possible. No vision is tantamount to misery, suffering, violence and death. Our violent society above all shows an atrophy of vision. Because there is no vision, people take to drugs. Because there is no vision, people explode with violence.

God is one of the good visions of man. Peace is a good vision. War is a bad vision. Selfish life is a bad vision. Bad visions spell out bad Dharmas.

May we have enough vision and strength to cultivate good visions. May our visions bring us to light. May light deepen our visions. May we use our visions to elevate the world and our own life.

Chapter 16

THE KEY TO HAPPINESS

Do not strive for happiness. You can only arrive at happiness while striving for other things. Happiness is not a fixed state of being; it is a state of perpetual becoming. Happiness cannot be designed. When happiness arrives you are no longer conscious of striving for it.

What should you strive for? The meaning in life, for the fulfilment that goes beyond your individual egoistic self. You are as great as the causes you aspire to. Great causes elevate you and make you transcend your small self. Great causes pervade you with reverence and infuse you with dignity, which are necessary components of a worthy life. Stretch yourself to the maximum in the service of others, in the cause of altruism. Merge with the larger scheme of things by understanding that the human destiny is made of the stars and not only of ordinary clay. And then your life will be enhanced, your being enlarged. And perhaps as a by product you will arrive at happiness.

What is happiness? The equilibrium of your being which is recognized by others as a state of serenity that is inspiring and uplifting; which is felt by you as a state of inner tranquillity that gives you strength and determination; not a state of sensual satisfaction or a state of physical comfort but a state of inner radiance which you will recognise more and more as you approach it closer and closer. Happiness is being at peace with yourself while the self is united with a larger order of things.

The truly blessed people, the giants of human thought and spirit, the Gandhis and the Schwetizers did not search for happiness, yet we find their lives radiant and inspiring - full to the brim in the service of great causes, in the service of others, in the service of large ideals which alone make sense of human destinies.

The concept of happiness should be abandoned for it is a trap usually concealing an ego trip. The key to happiness is to lose your ego and ambition, and to acquire a vision and a mission.

Chapter 17

CELEBRATING LIFE

The poet Shelley pronounces; "Poets are the gigantic mirrors in which futurity casts its shadow over the present." This is a fantastic insight. I will allow myself to parapharse Shelley and say: "Poets are the gigantic mirrors in which the deepest human aspirations find expression and articulation." This is in harmony with another statement of Shelley: "Poets are the unacknowledged legislators of humanity."

There is perhaps no more subtle and ravishing expression of the celebration of life than that of William Blake's:

> To see a world in a grain of sand
> And a heaven in the wild flower
> Hold infinity in the palm of your hand
> And eternity in an hour.

This is so simple and so mystical; and so magnificent in acknowledging our participation in the wonders of the becoming of the world. It was Blake also who said: "To the eye of the man of imagination, Nature is Imagination itself." It would be impudent at this point not to quote John Keats: "I feel more and more every day, as my imagination strengthens."

These various poets, I mentioned, are a much better source for the sustenance of life and for its celebration than either philosophers or scientists. It is entirely strange: No rational argument can convince you to be positive towards life. Science cannot explain what celebrating is. It does not have the language for it. Add 'celebratory' to the idea of the cosmos and you receive one sense of the universe. Take away the sense of celebration and you dwell in a rather shabby universe.

True, science does not support the idea of the celebratory universe or of celebrating life. But it cannot deny it either. At best science must be mute about such matters. Furthermore, there are more things in heaven and on earth than scientists ever dreamt in their theories.

To think is to celebrate.
To be alive is to celebrate.
To be aware of one's human nature is to celebrate.
To reach out for God is to celebrate.
To dance under the stars is to celebrate.
So my friend, go and celebrate.
For it is in congruence with the ethos of the universe.

Chapter 18

POEMS

Why
Be
Less?

You were born into the human form
Not for nothing.
The flowers can blossom radiantly,
But only you can embrace God.

Your Mind Divine
Can see in the lotus flower
The smiling Buddha.
You can re-live the past,
You can conjure up the future.
You can make yourself
Into Light Extraordinary.
You can..... but will you?

Most of you are prepared
To settle for much less.
But why be less
Than you were created for?

Dharma

The commands of the soul
To ascend higher and higher.

The call of one's mission.
To perform one's duty with joy.

The sense of responsibility
For the world and for oneself.

The challenge of wisdom.
To transcend knowledge;
The challenge of enlightenment
To transcend wisdom.

The light of understanding
To be human
To serve others
To serve the divine.

The response to the cries
Of Mother Earth and future generations
To protect and heal and love
So that all shall blossom
And all shall rejoice in being.